Making, Out

Making, Out

Plays by Gay Men

David Demchuk

Ken Garnhum

Sky Gilbert

Daniel MacIvor

Harry Rintoul

Colin Thomas

Edited by Robert Wallace

Coach House Press

Toronto

These plays are fully protected under the copyright laws of
Canada and all other countries of the Copyright Union and
are subject to royalty. Changes to a script are expressly
forbidden without written consent of the author. Rights to
produce, film, record in whole or in part, in any medium or
in any language, by any group, *amateur or professional,* are
retained by the authors. Interested persons are requested to
write to the address given prior to each play in order to
apply for permission and terms.

The punctuation of these plays carefully adheres
to the authors' instructions.

Published with the assistance of the Canada Council,
the Ontario Arts Council and the Ontario Ministry
of Culture and Communications.

Canadian Cataloguing in Publication Data
Main entry under title:

Making, out : plays by gay men

ISBN 0-88910-434-4

1. Canadian drama (English) -20th century.*
2. Gays' writings, Canadian (English) .*
I. Wallace, Robert, 1943-

PS8309.H67M35 1992   C812'.54080353   C92-093315-7
PR9196.7.H57M35 1992

To the memory of Michael Lynch
— poet, teacher, gay activist, friend

Contents

Acknowledgments

Thanks to Buddies In Bad Times Theatre, Tarragon Theatre, Theatre Direct and *Canadian Theatre Review* for their help in obtaining production photographs and histories.

Special thanks to Helena Van Nooten for her help in preparing the manuscript.

Ken Garnhum, *Beuys Buoys Boys:*

Grateful acknowledgment is made to Urjo Kareda, Andy McKim, Don Hannah, J.D. Prentice and Marta Stothers.

The playwright quotes:

Beckett, Samuel. *Endgame.* New York: Grove Press, 1958.

————. *Happy Days.* London: Faber & Faber, 1961.

————. *Waiting for Godot.* London: Faber & Faber, 1956.

Brecht, Bertolt. *Mother Courage and Her Children.* Translated by John Willett. London: Methuen, 1980.

Heger, Heinz. *The Men with the Pink Triangle.* Translated by David Fernbach. London: GMP, 1972.

Shakespeare, William. *King Lear.* In *The Complete Signet Classic Shakespeare.* New York: Harcourt Brace Jovanovich, 1972.

Daniel MacIvor, *2-2-Tango:*

It is a great pleasure for me to have *2-2-Tango* published in this collection of gay plays by gay men, and I would like to thank Ken McDougall for his belief in the project from the outset, Steve Cumyn for his great contribution to the original production, and Robin Fulford for his involvement as a producer in the original production.

Harry Rintoul, *Brave Hearts:*

I have to thank everyone at Buddies In Bad Times: Tim, Gwen, Clinton, everyone on the board, and all those I never met, Brian Henderson (especially Brian) for keeping me sane, telling me not to worry, and being a good person, but most of all I have to thank Sky for taking the risk of producing a new play, a prairie play, a naturalistic play; for allowing *Brave Hearts* to be more than just another 'workshopped' play. As well my thanks to Doug Arrell for his support and hard work, thanks to David Demchuk for the late-night phone calls and encouragement, thanks to Rory and MAP, who are always there, and last but not least to Kelly Wilson, Jonathan Barrett, and Brian Drader, who made it come off the page.

The playwright quotes:
Kennedy, William. *The Ink Truck.* New York: Viking, 1985.

Colin Thomas, *Flesh and Blood:*

I thank all of the artists and administrative staff, everyone involved in the original Theatre Direct production, for the sometimes extraordinary depth of their talent, and for their faith in the project. These individuals nurtured this script and their hearts are reflected in its pages.

Deepest thanks are also due to the many men (and a few women) who helped me write this play by sharing generously their intimate stories.

Making Out Positions

An Introduction

'Men who write openly as gay men have [...] often been excluded from the consensus of the traditional canon and may operate more forcefully now within a specifically gay/lesbian canon.' — Eve Kosofsky Sedgwick

To begin his recent essay 'Fresh Canons: The Native Canadian Example,' Terry Goldie notes that, 'Today, in the face of a variety of changes in value, literary institutions recognize the need to respond to what are perceived to be new bodies of literature' (373). Using texts by Native Canadians as his example, Goldie proceeds to discuss processes of canonization—the ways by which certain texts are established as important in a culture while others are not. The issues he raises are typical of many that currently disturb literature departments across the country. During the eighties, these issues were of primary interest to teachers in charge of curriculum development. Now, they not only pepper the literary pages of newspapers, magazines, and scholarly journals, but also enliven television debates.[1] In this climate of canonical enquiry, publishers who both service and construct readerships are fair game for interrogation. And when publishers are fair game, editors—particularly those with the power to choose texts— become sitting ducks.

Why are some texts regularly included in educational curricula and others not? Why do many English departments privilege British or American texts over those written by Canadian authors, especially Native Canadian ones? Why do literary canons invariably include more work by men than women, or by whites than blacks? Why is writing by Asian people so hard to find in libraries and schools?

One of the easiest ways to answer such questions is to note that curricular choices depend on the availability of books which, in turn, depends on publishing decisions. Canadian texts can replace American ones only when they are published—a fact that Canadian publishers struggle to impress upon governments that insist on the efficacy of free trade and book taxation despite their debilitating effects on the indigenous publishing industry. Similarly, for schools to introduce more texts by women, blacks, and visible minorities into their curricula, the books must first exist.

This also applies to invisible minorities such as lesbian women and gay men—which is a primary reason for publishing *Making, Out: Plays by Gay Men*. This book makes available, in a clear and unambiguous manner, work by an invisible minority that usually is ignored in mainstream curricula. The title foregrounds the sexual preference of the writers whose plays are included. In an unequivocal gesture, it links homosexuality (or, more correctly, 'gayness,') to the process of making plays—a statement I can make about very few books published in Canada today.

It is the writers in this book who are gay, not the plays—although all of these plays contain representations of gay men. Some of the writers (Garnhum, Gilbert, MacIvor, and Thomas) have performed these or similar characters in theatres themselves. Those who haven't also 'perform' by being 'out' as gay men in their everyday lives. To be more precise: all the writers in this book, by publicly declaring they are gay, contribute as much to the social sense of 'gayness' as do the gay characters they create.

Through their lives and their work, these writers help to construct gay subjectivities in Canada—a process that occurs both inside and out of the theatre.[2]

These writers share the activity of making out gay subjectivities; to me, this is more important than the differences that separate them from other gay men. Perhaps, if I were not only gay but black, I would not be able to say this so easily; perhaps if I weren't a writer, I wouldn't say it so readily. But I do privilege the experience that unites gay writers who make, out in public— privilege it over the differences that distinguish us from each other. In saying this, I do not mean to suggest that 'gayness' is a unified or monolithic identity. Rather, I consider it to be a circumstance that is affected by a significant number of material conditions.

There are infinite ways in which a person can be gay, just as there are many influences that affect how (and if) a gay person lives. 'Representative' images of gay people are as impossible to create as representative images of 'ordinary' men and women; invariably, those that attempt to be 'all-inclusive' sink to stereotypical clichés or worse. The writers of these plays are not gay in the same way as I am, even though they also are white, anglophone Canadians. Just as I don't endorse some of the positions they represent in their plays, I suspect they won't agree with all of my thoughts in this essay. Yet each of us shares one thing in common: we're all out.

In the Preface to *Gay Spirit: Myth and Meaning,* Mark Thompson specifies that 'the word *gay* should not be confused with *homosexual,*' explaining that '*Gay* implies a social identity and consciousness actively chosen, while *homosexual* refers to a specific form of sexuality. A person may be homosexual, but that does not necessarily imply that he or she would be gay' (xi). In agreeing with Thompson I do not deny that homosexual behaviour affects the way I constitute my subjectivity (my inner 'self') or my sex life. Rather, I reject 'homosexuality' as an arbitrary and misleading term extrapolated from biological discourse and applied to people with my 'orientation' by sexologists and psychiatrists during the last century.[3] In doing this, I also align myself with the theoretical position that holds that 'any identity is founded relationally, constituted in reference to an exterior or outside that defines the subject's own interior boundaries and corporeal surfaces' (Fuss 1991, 2). In 'Queer Theory: Lesbian and Gay Sexualities,' Teresa de Lauretis explains a central premise of this position: 'homosexuality is no longer to be seen simply as marginal with regard to a dominant, stable form of sexuality (heterosexuality) against which it would be defined either by opposition or by homology. [...] Instead, male and female homosexualities—in their current sexual-political articulations of gay and lesbian sexualities, in North America—may be reconceptualized as social and cultural forms in their own right, albeit emergent ones and thus still fuzzily defined, undercoded, or discursively dependent on more established forms' (iii).

The etymology of the word 'gay' is obscure. Probably, the word is related to the French word 'gai' that was used as early as the thirteenth or fourteenth centuries to denote an openly homosexual person.[4] In this century, it began to be used similarly during the late sixties and early seventies when, as George Stambolian puts it, 'a generation ... after decades of repression could celebrate its new consciousness and the very fact that it was creating a new culture on its own terms' (5). In *More Man than You'll Ever Be*, Joseph P. Goodwin explains why the distinction between the words 'homosexual' and 'gay' is important in a way that makes sense to me. 'Occasional homosexual acts may be performed by heterosexual people,' he writes in his introduction; '*Gay*, however, is a self-identification, used consciously by those homosexual people who are accepting of their sexual orientation, but it extends beyond the mere sexual aspects of life.' Later Goodwin observes that, 'The gay subculture is made up of those homosexual people who have identified themselves as gay, who consider their orientations to be an important (but not totally defining) aspect of their lives, and who frequently interact with gays *as* gays' (xii).

Obviously, it is not necessary to 'come out' in order to interact with gay men. But for a man to interact with gay men *as gay*, at least with any frequency, it probably is inevitable. Diana Fuss eloquently theorizes the process of coming out as 'a movement into a metaphysics of presence, speech, and cultural visibility' (1991, 4). In part she develops a simple idea—that coming out initiates a change in (self-)consciousness, a re-thinking or re-making of individual subjectivity that responds to the radical reorganization of everyday life necessitated by declaring one's difference from the norm. While this can have positive social effects, allowing, as Jeffrey Weeks puts it, 'the "sexual outlaws" of old [to construct] a way of life, or more accurately ways of life, which have reversed the expectations of sexology' (200) it can be extremely difficult, stressful, and downright dangerous for people living in a heterosexist society.

The out gay man, no matter what his race, class, age, or education, shares a common experience in most parts of the world. This experience is homophobia, an irrational dread of homosexuality, that precipitates an ugly range of subtle through savage attacks on lesbian women and gay men in a wide variety of cultures. Certainly this is the case for out gay men living in Canada today. Fear and loathing of homosexuality is so rampant in contemporary Canadian society that it even transcends gender: the out gay *person*, whether male or female, invariably shares the same experience of injustice and ostracization that homophobia breeds.[5] Which leads to another reason for publishing this book.

A number of these plays, besides celebrating gay lives, reveal the homophobia that gay people confront every day, and they expose the havoc that homophobia wreaks on both individuals and societies. Like gayness itself, homophobia is invisible until it is manifest in action: to the extent that some of the plays in this collection depict homophobic activity, the book also makes this insidious force visible. Because the power of homophobia is so strong, it frequently is internalized by gay men themselves, a fact illustrated by the character of Rafe in Harry Rintoul's *Brave Hearts*. The representation of self-oppression is a useful strategy for defeating it—particularly if, as in Rintoul's play, a self-hating gay man is embraced with love by another. The ending of this play could only be envisioned by a brave heart—in this case, by a gay man who dares to be so romantic as to suggest that love can not only conquer hate; it also can defy death.

A different form of homophobia is expressed by the character of Allan, the heterosexual teenager in Colin Thomas's *Flesh and Blood* who must face the fact that his brother is gay and has AIDS. Potentially, this representation of homophobia is more useful than the one in *Brave Hearts* if only because it is central to a play conceived for adolescents. Originally commissioned by Vancouver's Green Thumb Theatre, a company that produces work for young audiences, the play was abandoned by the theatre when B.C.'s health ministry withdrew funding for the project. In an interview with the *Toronto Star*, Thomas notes that he 'wasn't that surprised that the Social Credit government, with a born-again health minister, wasn't going to support the show.' In the same interview he also states that while he realizes it would have been safer for him to deal with the issues surrounding 'safe sex' in a heterosexual context, 'as a gay man, I'm so tired of being sensitive to the dominant sensibility' (Wagner 1991, 'Frank,' B3).

No wonder Colin Thomas is tired. The dominant sensibility of Canadian culture is as anti-sexual as it is homophobic—which no doubt compounded the difficulty of producing *Flesh and Blood* in which the adolescent characters, as well as the gay ones, are sexually intimate. But, I suspect it was Thomas's linkage of homophobia with fundamentalist religion that posed the biggest problems for B.C.'s minister of health. The attitudes of the Social Credit government towards health and education were as conservative as its fiscal policies. And, as Cindy Patton explains in her book *Inventing AIDS*, 'homophobia is still something that few *progressive* [my emphasis] people will put on their agenda, and is rarely perceived as something they "might have." At best, homophobia merits a one shot consciousness-raising event, or is added to the end of a long list of oppressions or demands for civil rights' (111).

Flesh and Blood eventually was produced for teenage audiences by Toronto's Theatre Direct—'the only other company in Canada that would touch this script' (Wagner 1991, 'Frank,' B3)—and remounted the following year for a run partially subsidized by the City of Toronto's Board of Health. Evidently, city officials were as impressed as I was by the excitement generated by the Toronto production of the play. Not only were the young people in the audience engaged by the performance, they were eager to talk about the issues it raised in the post-show discussions with the director and cast. Most of them appeared to be seeing live representations of themselves for the first time. Listening to them talk about the novelty of seeing 'themselves' on stage, I was struck with the similarity between their situation and that of gay men and lesbians, as well as a host of visible minorities. Until recently, all of us have been excluded from theatrical representation except when we are necessary to complete the narratives of 'adult,' white, heterosexual culture.

Traditionally, when children or adolescents are represented on stage, they are presented from the adult's point of view. Similarly, gay characters are constructed through the heterosexual (male) gaze in most of the drama that is taught in universities and produced on the main stages of Canadian theatres. This also is true for people of colour and, as feminists now have made very clear, for women as well. As I watched the students react enthusiastically to the performance of *Flesh and Blood,* I realized yet again how Canadian theatre so often perpetuates the biases of our dominant cultures and how, in doing so, it constructs a false representation of our society that excludes a very large audience.

Just as adolescent characters rarely are represented on stage, the sex lives of gay characters rarely are represented as unproblematic.[6] Gay characters hardly ever fuck. This is not the case for the gay characters presented in this book. In all the plays in this collection, the gay characters have sex or, at least, talk about having it—in positive though complex ways. This is another reason I chose these plays and one of the reasons I created the book's title. Quite simply, I wanted to publish a sex-positive book in this country where sexual activity, let alone gay sex, is regularly represented in a negative manner. Making out—without the comma—is as common a term as the activity it signifies; making out on stage, however, is rare.

Perhaps this is why David Demchuk's rather 'slight' play, *Touch,* caused such a 'heavy' commotion when it premiered in 1986 at the annual *Rhubarb!* festival sponsored by Buddies In Bad Times Theatre, a Toronto company that produces innovative gay and lesbian theatre. Two nude men slip under a rumpled sheet covering a mattress and proceed to discuss the role of pornography in their lives and imaginations. Their almost Platonic dialogue is staged in an atmosphere of homoerotic intimacy that works as a paradigm for the questions about representation and arousal that they debate. This is sex-play with intelligence, titillation with redeeming social value. The central irony of this very ironic play is that the characters' ideological positions are overshadowed by the actors' physical positions in bed. In effect, the actors perform for the audience an example of the erotics at issue. If the audience agrees with Ken who opposes the uses of erotic representation, it must question its voyeuristic position in the theatre. If it agrees with Gary who views pornography as useful, where does it draw the line? Would the audience watch these two nude men do more than talk? If not, why not? Questions about making out become questions about making, out.

It is unlikely that *Touch* will make it into university curricula, just as it is unlikely that *Flesh and Blood* will be included in the curriculum of B.C.'s secondary schools—which is a shame, given that the insight and brevity that Demchuk brings to the topic of gay male pornography would make *Touch* an ideal text for discussion in a number of different disciplines. But just as condoms are considered too radical to distribute in prisons, I suspect that plays that present same-sex possibilities, let alone same-sex imagery, are considered too radical for post-secondary students—at least by those currently responsible for determining the curricula used in Canadian universities. Which brings me back to issues of canonicity.

Although plays by gay men *are* taught in literature courses at universities across the country (plays, for example, by Edward Albee, Noel Coward, Jean Genet, Tomson Highway, Joe Orton, Michel Tremblay, Oscar Wilde, and Tennessee Williams), rarely are they approached as the work of gay men whose particular experience of the world—experience that is affected by their homosexuality—might impact on how and what they write. One of the reasons for this is simple: when an author's homosexuality isn't immediately evident, it need not be discussed. As Robert K. Martin writes in his introduction to *The Homosexual Tradition in American Poetry*, 'Most writing has traditionally been heterosexual, not by declaration but by implication. Men and women are assumed to be heterosexual until proved otherwise. And heterosexual assumptions are presumed to be universal' (1979, xv-xvi). The consequence of this is that work by gay men can be appropriated by the dominant culture and interpreted exclusively within a heterosexual context.

Arguably, ignoring the author's sexuality, like ignoring the author's gender, has little effect on his or her text, the text being 'neutral' until it is invested with meaning by a reader. A text will (simply) mean differently if it is contextualized within the frames of sexuality or gender than if it is not. In this line of reasoning (which constitutes a theory of reading[7]), the idea of a 'gay text' is problematic. If 'gayness' is a relational identity independent of essential or innate characteristics—a social construction that undergoes 'shifts' through a process of continuous reinvention—a text is even more so. Until it is interpreted by readers, a text has no meaning except to its author. And even when it is read, its meaning is specific to individual readers or 'reading communities'—is, in other words, a construction between readers, a negotiation.[8]

For this reason I take issue with the idea of a 'gay play.' While I may consider all the plays in this volume to be gay, someone else may not. Are these plays 'gay' because they depict gay characters? If so, does a play require gay characters to fit the category? What about Oscar Wilde's *The Importance of Being Earnest* or *Le Balcon* by Jean Genet, two plays that I would want to discuss in relation to their authors' homosexuality (and would possibly term 'gay'), but neither of which contains any gay characters? Is a play about gay men automatically a gay play? Certainly I can think of a number of plays about gay men that are written by men who are *not* gay that might qualify—plays such as *Streamers* by David Rabe or *Steel Kiss* by Robin Fulford. Does an author's sexuality even affect his or her ability to write a gay or lesbian play? Can only a gay man write a gay play? This question poses another which is even more problematic: can a gay man write only gay plays? If so, what about Tomson Highway's *The Rez Sisters* or Michel Tremblay's *Les Belles-Soeurs*—plays that present, almost exclusively, female, heterosexual characters? Are these gay plays?

But let me bring these questions directly to bear on this book. On its back cover, Vit Wagner, a theatre critic for the *Toronto Star*, suggests that in *2-2-Tango*, playwright Daniel

MacIvor's 'observations about the eternal struggle in relationships between emotional, physical, and spiritual need and the assertion of independence easily exceed the gay context in which they are being played out' (Wagner 1991, 'Gay,' D14). What does Wagner mean? That a play about the mating rituals of two gay characters, whose stylized actions and overlapping speech clearly signify their fictivity, is a play about any two people who meet, make out, and break up? If so, doesn't it follow that a play about the mating trauma enacted by two heterosexual characters—in, say, a play like *Talley's Folly* (which is written by a gay man, Lanford Wilson)—also could 'transcend its context' to become a play about gay men? If this is the case, what, then, is a gay play? Or, for that matter, what isn't? When a gay man reads a text, who knows what he'll find? That *Who's Afraid of Virginia Woolf?* is 'really' about two gay male couples? That the prostitutes in *Le Balcon* are 'really' gay men in drag? Perhaps Vit Wagner could find that Mart Crowley's *The Boys in the Band* transcends its gay context to suggest a Tupperware party for suburban housewives? Perhaps *I* could!

Such questions inevitably lead to a discussion of the writer's 'voice': can a man write a woman, a woman write a man? Can a white man write a black man, a black man an Asian? Can an adult write a child, a non-Native a Native? These questions are especially important to playwrights for whom 'voice' is always a practical as well as theoretical matter. Most playwrights create characters who not only speak but who do so in social contexts that simulate an experience of the world. Moreover, these characters are interpreted by actors whose representations usually are determined by the words given to them by the author. Because most playwrights create work that relies on conflict to generate dramatic tension, the differences that distinguish people are an important creative resource in their writing. This is particularly the case for gay playwrights who wish to represent the ways in which gay people are constructed as different by the societies in which they exist. But it also applies to any playwright concerned to represent the ways in which 'difference' affects human existence.

In *Essentially Speaking*, Diana Fuss argues against 'the authority of experience,' particularly as it is used in the classroom. 'Exactly what counts as "experience,"' she asks, 'and should we defer to it in pedagogical situations? Does experience of oppression confer special jurisdiction over the right to speak about that oppression? Can we only speak, ultimately, from the so-called "truth" of our experiences, or are all empirical ways of knowing analytically suspect' (113)? Although Fuss effectively challenges the experience-based position as 'essentialist,' she nevertheless is careful to protect it from abuse: 'The anti-essentialist displacement of experience must not be used as a convenient means of silencing students, no matter how shaky experience has proven to be as a basis of epistemology' (1989, 117).

My own position on this matter is similar to Fuss's. For me, the reductivist position that holds that only a gay man can write a gay man, a Native woman write a Native woman etc., is not just limiting to the playwright but anathematic to creative expression and cross-cultural understanding. I am not a gay 'nationalist' interested in establishing a distinct society for which only gay men and lesbian women can speak. Nevertheless, I am sympathetic to the tactics of the reductivist position to the degree that they strategize cultural preservation, if only because I have seen how the appropriation of voice can effectively disempower people who need to speak in their own terms.

My primary hope for this book is that it will stimulate discussion of the relations between gay subjectivities, representation, and reading. The book responds to the silence that currently surrounds the work of gay men and lesbian women in the institutions of Canadian culture. Nowhere is this silence more deafening than in the classrooms of Canadian universities in which students study English. The gay or lesbian student who looks to texts for a representation, if not a validation, of his or her experience is abused by both the curricula and the pedagogy that prevails in most departments of English. Rather than help this student discover something about herself in the text—an avowed aim of progressive pedagogy—most approaches to texts written by lesbian and gay authors all but eliminate the possibility. The avoidance of gay readings affirms the heterosexual assumption that routinely frames the discussion of texts in Canadian schools. This does more than appropriate the work of gay writers: it effaces gay life.

Where is the gay student to find representations of his or her subjectivity except in texts that are overtly positioned as the work of gay writers? While this question is extremely important, I have explained how another is more crucial. What must be the position of the teacher who respects the lived experience of her students at the same time that she views this experience as the construction of social and historical contexts? The question becomes more complex when the teacher is gay. How do I facilitate gay readings of texts by gay men without privileging them over others? And how, if I allow these readings, do I problematize them as unstable constructions—interpretations that are relational to historical and material conditions?

Obviously, these questions implicate this book as well as critical pedagogy; and they inform this essay which, by now, possibly seems to present contradictory positions. At this point, I must candidly acknowledge that I haven't discovered ways of answering these questions that are consistent, cohesive, and complete. But, I must add (and I consider it an important qualification), I don't think I want to. I am skeptical of uniform and unitary positions that facilitate 'correct' notions of speech, interpretation, and behaviour—no matter from where they issue. As a result, I can align myself with Diana Fuss who summarizes her stance on these matters at the end of *Essentially Speaking* in this way:

> ... we need both to theorize essentialist spaces from which to speak and, simultaneously, to deconstruct these spaces to keep them from solidifying. Such a double gesture involves once again the responsibility to historicize, to examine each deployment of essence, each appeal to experience, each claim to identity in the complicated contextual frame in which it is made. (118)

To be simpler about this, we must admit what we don't know, just as we must acknowledge that each person knows differently. This would be an especially refreshing pedagogical approach for teachers for whom the traditions of lesbian and gay representation are as foreign as the signifying practices of lesbian and gay life.[9] As Cindy Patton notes, 'While liberals are discovering they have gay/ lesbian friends and colleagues, few non-gay/lesbian people have much exposure to the diverse cultural and social life of the lesbian and gay community' (111). The dominant culture easily deals with its inability to discuss what it doesn't know or understand—or what it condemns as immoral, abnormal, or sick: it ignores it and, in an instant, eradicates difference. This common strategy for displacing the 'other' is a central mechanism of the process of marginalization in which potentially dissident groups are silenced before they can begin to speak. To overcome it, we must do more than challenge publishing priorities and rethink university curricula. We also must reassess pedagogical practice and expose its ideological assumptions.

What is at stake in the classroom is personal autonomy: the right of an individual to declare that his or her position/perception is distinctively important. Traditional canons, like the other received institutions of Canadian culture, militate against this autonomy by prescribing the importance of inherited texts to teachers and students alike. But how can their pernicious influence be overcome when, as Terry Goldie explains, a canon 'is an institutional inevitability, whether that institution is "literature" or the university.' Goldie offers one method: the constant surveillance of the means by which canons are perpetuated. He suggests that canons 'be under constant examination as a balance of powers. [...] Not the canon itself but the strategies through which we all explore canonization' (383). Invariably such scrutiny would require editors and teachers to examine their reasons for positioning certain texts as valuable; and it would demand that they consider that other texts might be equally important but for different reasons.

In another essay on canonicity, Robert K. Martin puts this more personally: 'I think we owe it to our students to present the assumptions that underlie our questions as well as the answers that may follow from them' (1991, 393). Later in the same essay, Martin poses a question on behalf of the many teachers (and students) who, like Vit Wagner, probably will view this pedagogical strategy with skepticism: 'Where is that splendid transcendent position where all difference evaporates,' Martin asks. He supplies his own answer: 'Wherever it is, it's out of politics, which is precisely what needs to be brought back into the classroom' (1991, 394).

Politics, I suggest, has never left the classroom; rather, it's been lingering in the hall, poking its nose through the door whenever it gets a chance. Certainly this is the case of gay politics, for which the closet is still a more appropriate metaphor than a common corridor. Indeed, for Eve Kosofsky Sedgwick, gay politics and pedagogy go hand-in-hand. As she explains in *The Epistemology of the Closet*, homosexuality is the 'open secret' imbedded in the master canons of Western culture—the homosexuality of many writers being the context that goes unspoken in the teaching of 'great' books. To her questions, 'Has there ever been a gay Socrates ... a gay Shakespeare ... a gay Proust?' Sedgwick replies, 'not only have there been a gay Socrates, Shakespeare, and Proust but ... their names are Socrates, Shakespeare, Proust; and beyond that, legion—dozens or hundreds of the most centrally canonic figures in what monoculturalists are pleased to consider "our" culture, as indeed, always in different forms and senses, in every other' (1990, *Epistemology*, 52).

Sedgwick begins her book with the provocation that, 'an understanding of virtually any aspect of modern Western culture must be, not merely incomplete, but damaged in its central substance to the degree that it does not incorporate a critical analysis of modern homo/heterosexual definition.' She then states boldly that 'the appropriate place for that critical analysis to begin is from the relatively decentered perspective of modern gay and anti-homophobic theory' (1990, *Epistemology*, 1). For her, the project and practice of gay theory will lead not only to the dismantlement of the official tradition—'the naming as what it is of a hegemonic, homoerotic/homophobic male canon of cultural mastery and coercive erotic double-binding'—but also to the 're-creation of minority gay canons from currently noncanonical material' (1990, *Epistemology*, 58).

As I indicated at the beginning of this essay, the 'naming' of hegemonic canons is now well begun. The process of recuperating the homosexual writers within these canons also is underway. In his 1979 book, *The Homosexual Tradition in American Poetry*, Robert K. Martin links the work of Walt Whitman and Hart Crane to that of Allen Ginsberg, Robert Duncan, Thom Gunn, James Merrill, and other, lesser known American poets to delineate a tradition that rests on these writers' 'sense of a shared sexuality' and their 'references to earlier gay writers.' Martin considers this tradition to have evolved 'partly out of a need for communication (in which allusions can serve as code references) and partly out of a feeling of exclusion from the traditions of male heterosexual writing' (1979, xv).

Until the 1970s, most gay and lesbian playwrights, like gay people in general, were unable to openly declare themselves as gay for fear of social recrimination and artistic censure. In many instances, this inability affected their plays, leading them to create what Graham Jackson calls a 'theatre of implication' in which overt representations of homosexual behaviour were limited or disguised.[10] Since the advent of gay/lesbian liberation in the late sixties, this situation has improved as more gay men and lesbians have dared to become visible and vocal in all areas of life. Despite increased visibility, progress towards equality, let alone acceptance, is slow. In *Culture Clash: The Making of Gay Sensibility*, Michael Bronski explains some of the reasons for this. 'Gay liberation ... brought not only gay people, but also homophobia, out of the closet. Lesbians and gay men were easy targets for hatred. This homophobia was particularly noticeable in the politics and the literature of the New Right. By pronouncing homosexuality to be antithetical to traditional sexual values, gender roles, and the family the right was able to use gay visibility and homophobic fears for its own political ends' (4). Since the advent of AIDS, this has become even more the case, as Cindy Patton explains in *Inventing AIDS:*

> The non gay/lesbian world collapses all of the gay/lesbian community's experience into that embodied by people living with AIDS. While the plight of people living with AIDS is very real, so are the effects of homophobia which work both in tandem with AIDS-related discrimination and independently. AIDS-related discrimination furthermore operates in tandem with sexism and racism, which were accepted as valid social concerns before AIDS, while gay/lesbian concerns have only been marginally legitimated, and only in relation to AIDS. Demands for the civil rights and cultural autonomy of lesbians and gay men are seen as 'politicizing' AIDS or as manipulating AIDS policy for an unrelated gay rights agenda. (111)

For just such reasons, the Canadian publishing industry has been slow to respond to the proliferation of gay and lesbian communities that have developed during the last three decades. Because Canadian theatre also is reluctant to produce work that deals openly with gay interests and behaviour, texts by lesbians and gay men still enter Canadian culture through the back door. Canadian playwrights who openly declare a same-sex preference still are subject to enormous prejudice—systemic homophobia that works to silence voices that offer alternatives to the heterosexual norm. This is especially the case for lesbian women. To prove this statement, simply try to construct a list of lesbian playwrights similar to the list of gay male playwrights I cited earlier. How many lesbian women have their work produced on Canadian stages, published by Canadian publishers, and taught in Canadian universities?

Ten years ago, it was much more difficult to answer this question than it is today. Marie-Claire Blais, Audrey Butler, Lena Chartrand, Ann-Marie MacDonald, Jovette Marchessault: the list of Canadian female playwrights who have chosen to declare their sexual preference is growing quickly. But because a man can declare his homosexuality more easily than a woman in our patriarchal society, the list of Canadian male playwrights who also have chosen to come out is lengthening faster. Now, Michel Marc Bouchard, Normand Chaurette, René-Daniel Dubois, Brad Fraser, Don Hannah, Bryden MacDonald, Kent Stetson, Raymond Storey, and Allan Stratton have joined such early pioneers as John Herbert, Larry Fineberg, John Palmer, and Michel Tremblay by coming out as gay men in interviews and features carried by the mass media. Along with the six playwrights in this book, they construct a lineage of gay male playwrights whose work has been both produced and published in Canada—work that can constitute a Canadian gay theatrical tradition.

It is not my purpose in this introduction to define the

parameters of this tradition or to distil its conventions. Rather, I want to acknowledge that it exists—and to celebrate its central and crucial contribution to Canadian theatre. As a gay man, I am proud to be able to publish these plays and to position them openly as plays by gay men. I am especially pleased that some of them overtly acknowledge gay male traditions of art, theatre, and writing and, in so doing, connect with the work of gay writers in other cultures and different times.

The work of gay artists from outside Canada has played a central role in Sky Gilbert's writing since he first began producing his own plays in 1979, the year he co-founded Buddies In Bad Times Theatre in Toronto. Cavafy, Cocteau, David Hockney, Robert Mapplethorpe, Frank O'Hara, Pasolini: in *Capote at Yaddo*, Gilbert's representation of the young Truman Capote joins this long list of gay men whose lives and work continue to stimulate his creativity and to construct his gay subjectivity. It is appropriate that Gilbert's 'very gay little musical,' as he subtitles the piece, focuses on Capote's effect on other writers—specifically, Howard Doughty and Newton and Mary Arvin—given that Gilbert has so directly incorporated the history and work of other gay men into his plays. Much of his work for the theatre illustrates the way that intertexts create traditions in art; more importantly, it perpetuates and adds to gay male ones.

The intertexts in Gilbert's work are as much formal as thematic. In *Capote at Yaddo*, for instance, Gilbert's collaboration with composer John Alcorn results in a form of musical repartee that borrows from Noel Coward and Cole Porter. Similarly, his use of song to develop characterization suggests the work of Jerry Hermann, Stephen Sondheim, and Harvey Fierstein. Gilbert is a master of pastiche whose prolific creativity has led him to create what can be considered a typology of gay theatrical forms ranging from agitprop cartoon through camp parody to evocative *film noir* imagism. *Capote at Yaddo* presents him at his most urbane, its bright and witty style covering a sophisticated psychological study of a brilliant writer whose notoriety was his most fascinating creation.

The performance work of Ken Garnhum also uses intertexts to great effect. In his note on *Beuys Buoys Boys,* Garnhum states that he 'explores survival through the life and work of the German artist and humanist Joseph Beuys, through a childhood by the sea, and through a personal response to the AIDS epidemic.' It is important to know that Garnhum performed this piece when it premiered in Toronto—and, indeed, that he has performed all of his shows which, to date, have been conceived as solo works. In these pieces, Garnhum integrates his background as a visual artist with his love of painting, words, and ideas, transforming personal history into performative examples of making, out, things—or, to play with the words even further, making things out.

Perhaps more than any work in this collection, *Beuys Buoys Boys* is concerned with the artist's method and meaning of making things—with his constant need to translate his perceptions into tangible objects and events that communicate his interests and concerns. As Garnhum explains, his works 'deny singularity and insist on the connectedness of all things.' In *Beuys Buoys Boys,* he fashions this connectedness into a performance that is a memorial to the millions of gay men who lost their lives by being gay—an intertext of profound signification. Quoting from Heinz Heger's *The Men with the Pink Triangle,* Garnhum helps his audiences recognize that the variety of triangles he constructs on stage throughout his performance are symbols of both loss and survival—tributes to the gay men who have died because of various forms of oppression, and to those who, like himself, continue to live and make out in a homophobic world.

Towards the end of *Beuys Buoys Boys,* Ken Garnhum offers some remarks that have particular pertinence to the positions I have been developing in this essay:

... lately my understanding of survival has undergone a change. For instance, I have not just been ignoring, but I have actually been embracing the oppression that comes with being a gay man in this society. What I mean is—I feel so damn guilty about being a First World, white, able-bodied *male* person, that my oppression as a 'faggot' is almost welcome to me. It alleviates my guilt by making me a part of the oppressed masses.

At this time when plays by gay men are finally being published and gay and lesbian cultures are on the verge of birthing gay and lesbian studies, it is important that white, gay men reflect upon our privileges as much as our persecution. While this book is a breakthrough in Canadian publishing, in the United States it is simply one of many anthologies of work by gay men that have been published during the last fifteen years. Accompanying the remarkable proliferation of literature by American gay men and lesbians is a growing list of academic studies focused on the representation of gay men and lesbians in the novel, cinema, and mass culture, some of which I have quoted here.

The depth and breadth of this work is so considerable that Thomas Yingling, in an essay published in 1991, was able to posit that gay and lesbian literature has reached its 'canonical moment.' Rather than celebrate this moment, Yingling cautions that, 'We should not forget that canonical moments—in which the multiplicity of signification and desire is made coherent in and as a collective fantasy of origin—occur only at the expense of some repression' (186). Reviewing two recent books of gay theory, Yingling is led to a self-reflexivity not unlike Ken Garnhum's in *Beuys Buoys Boys*. He asks: 'What is forgotten in the drive to achieve institutional presence and in the privileging of male or female homosexuality as a distinct facet of human culture? How is the object of gay and lesbian studies to be constructed' (187)?

Yingling's questions lead him to worry that white gay men, in our rush to be published, produced, read, and discussed, will, by necessity, silence other minority voices less privileged than we by virtue of their race, gender or social position. I have not been unaware of this possibility in choosing to edit this book. I agree with Yingling that 'exactly what pressure lesbian and gay studies is to feel from "other" minority discourses is what should be at stake in constructing it as a distinct field ...' (191). But I also suggest that my self-consciousness about this issue, like Garnhum's—indeed, like Yingling's itself—indicates that the canonical moment has changed for those of us who can entertain its possibility. Such a moment is perpetually suspended, held like a frozen frame for us to inspect.

The time has passed for any minority to insist upon the specificity of its rights without considering 'the transformation of social relations as a whole' (Fredric Jameson, quoted in Yingling, 185). Those of us white, gay men who have achieved positions in which we can make ourselves seen, heard, and read as people making, out must accept the responsibility of questioning our power even as we exercise it. If we have achieved the moment when we can construct our traditions openly in public, we also have reached the point where we must deconstruct them to keep them effective. Only through such a 'double gesture' can our politics hope to displace the net of oppressions in which homophobia is just one string. We must look at ourselves looking, must watch ourselves making, must make self-consciousness a positive force in our subjectivities.

Moments of self-reflexivity are rare in Canadian theatre—if only because the types of plays being written today usually prevent the artist from speaking his or her feelings except through the mediation of characters—the standard convention of theatrical narrative. Even when this convention is parodied, as in Gilbert's 'camp' constructions such as *Lola Starr Builds Her Dream Home,* [11] it fails to achieve the same political efficacy as Garnhum's scripted

'confessions' in *Beuys Buoys Boys*. Directly addressing the audience, Garnhum publicly performs his own subjectivity (or makes
us think he does) by documenting his evolution as a gay man who
questions the privilege he feels as part of his social position.

A similar technique is developed in Daniel MacIvor's
2-2-Tango when MacIvor himself plays one of the two 'Jims' who
character the piece—as he did in both Toronto productions of the
play. In this almost cryptic work of performance, the two characters, identically clothed and closely matched in height, weight,
and grooming, perform an elegant mirror dance with the audience
as well as each other. Who's watching whom here? Just as each
character sees himself in the other, the audience finds a reflection
of itself in the couple's interactions. This is particularly the case for
those single gay men and lesbian women who regularly engage
in recreational sex. The dance metaphor that MacIvor uses to
propel the piece neatly plays with the routine steps of casual
encounters, as well as the variety of positions that same-sex
partners can assume in and out of bed. It is the recognition of this
that makes this piece so funny to an audience. The wit of the
writing is that it both precipitates and reflects the visual style of the
piece. Offering a verbal dance as elegant and light in its use of
repetition, staccato dialogue, and simultaneous speech as the
characters' soft-shoe routines, *2-2-Tango* presents gay men with
an image of themselves that is both sophisticated and self-
conscious. For me, this paradox of ingenuous cynicism gives the
play its dynamic edge.

Watching Daniel MacIvor or Ken Garnhum perform in their
own work, it is possible for the audience to conclude that the
actors/writers are 'playing' themselves—that the artists are
making, out in public. Partly, I think, this ambiguity accounts for
the interest generated by the Toronto productions of *2-2-Tango*
and, more generally, most of Daniel MacIvor's work. It also
accounts for the discomfort that some people feel when they find

themselves directly addressed by such a personal performer. Certainly this is the case for Garnhum whose work consistently wins more critical than commercial interest. And while it's no solace to the writer to suggest that this might be a compliment, I offer it nevertheless: work that openly confronts the audience with what it otherwise would ignore is vulnerable to neglect.

For me, making, out is synonymous with disruptive, energizing possibilities. Work that 'acts up' as deliberate and definite provocation also acts out the significance of gay subjectivities that are different from the norm. It reminds me of all those who have acted up before, and all those who couldn't—of all those for whom acting up meant an end and not a beginning. For those of us who have the power to create gay and lesbian work, the 'canonical moment' must be not only frozen, but fractured and fractious as well. Ken Garnhum concludes *Beuys Buoys Boys* with the lines: 'A memory is like a monument, it is a tricky thing; you have to find a place to put it. The site is all-important.' The men whose work is in this book have chosen to situate their monuments to gay lives in theatres—public spaces where memory can become that 'metaphysics of presence, speech and visibility' by which Diana Fuss terms coming out. This book is a monument too—to a point in the evolution of Canadian culture when gay men can begin to dismantle the canons of official tradition, not simply by constructing new ones, but by openly acknowledging the processes of canonicity. We are what we do; and what we do will determine who we become.

Robert Wallace, Toronto, February 1992

Endnotes:

1 For a comprehensive discussion of canonicity within the curricula of English departments in Canadian universities see 'The Canon and the Curriculum,' a special issue of the quarterly journal *English Studies in Canada*, vol. XVII, no. 4 (December 1991) in which Goldie's essay appears.

2 The subject of gay identity formation receives close scrutiny in *inside/out: Lesbian Theories, Gay Theories*, a collection of essays edited by Diana Fuss. In her introduction she writes: 'How, indeed, does one know if one is gay? The very insistence of the epistemological frame of reference in theories of homosexuality may suggest that we cannot know—surely or definitively. Sexual identity may be less a function of knowledge than performance, or, in Foucauldian terms, less a matter of final discovery than perpetual reinvention' (6-7).

3 In his introduction to *Gayspeak: Gay Male & Lesbian Communication*, James W. Chesebro writes: '*Homosexuality* is, after all, a biological term which specifies only that a physical sexual release can occur between members of the same sex. The word homosexual is a rather meaningless word as a social concept. It cannot tell us how, under what conditions, when, or why a homosexual acts; nor does the word specify a type of person or what the reactions to homosexual behaviour will be. Social customs, norms, and the rules governing homosexual behaviour are as varied as the number of persons engaged in such behaviour' (x-xi).

4 See Boswell, p. 43, note 6.

5 It is perhaps important to note that homophobia is no less rampant in the United States where the gay and lesbian movement has won greater attention, if not success, than in Canada. As recently as 1990, Eve Kosofsky Sedgwick, an American academic profoundly engaged in anti-homophobic work, writes in *The Epistemology of the Closet:* '… women and men who find or fear they are homosexual, or are perceived by others to be so, are physically and mentally terrorized through the institutions of law, religion, psychotherapy, mass culture, medicine, the military, commerce and bureaucracy, and brute violence. Political progress on these and similar life-and-death issues has depended precisely on the strength of a minority-model gay activism; it is the normalizing, persuasive analogy between the needs of gay/lesbian students and those of Black or Jewish students, for instance, and the development of the corresponding political techniques that enable progress in such arenas' (58).

6 It is interesting to consider that Mark Gevisser's comments about gay theatre in New York City might apply to the situation of theatre for young audiences as well as to theatre for gay men. He writes: 'Rites of definition occur in communities that do not consider themselves already defined or that are discontent with the way they have been defined by others. There is obviously no annual WASP Pride Day; there's no funky little theatrical space way up in the East 80s called the Straight-Boy Cafe where men can gather together to define and redefine a collective identity, because every commercial theatre is a Straight-Boy Cafe; every proscenium north of 14th Street frames a stable heterosexual white male identity that has been set in stone for centuries' (47).

7 This approach to reading, known as Reception Theory, considers that the interpretation of a text is a function of its readers and its reception. As Robert C. Holub explains in his useful introduction to the theory, 'The conception of an objective and eternal work of art with a unique structure and a single,

determinate meaning [is] replaced by a variety of models in which the essence of the work is a never-completed unfolding of its effective history, while its meaning is constituted by the interaction between text and reader' (148).

8 One of the main proponents of this point of view is the American theorist Stanley Fish, whose position Holub problematizes in his book. Holub explains that, 'To the questions: what does the reader then read? or what does the critic interpret? Fish has no answer. But he feels that no one else could answer these questions either, since any attempt to establish an objective essence independent of the reader, even it if were only black marks on a white page, would already be made from a position inside of an interpretive community. The text, in short, disappears at this metacritical level because Fish considers any statement about it to be informed by prior conventions of interpretation ...' (151). Where a reader learns these 'prior conventions,' of course, becomes a crucial question for critics of Reception Theory. For Roland Barthes and other post-structuralists, for example, the reader is himself a text as indeterminate as any other, whose 'competency' with interpretive conventions is constructed by the material conditions of history and society.

9 In using the term 'teachers,' I make a distinction between teachers working in post-secondary institutions (colleges and universities) and those teaching in elementary and secondary schools. Primarily, my remarks are addressed to teachers in post-secondary institutions who have much more freedom to discuss difference in the classroom than those who teach in secondary schools. Discussing this situation in the United States, Eve Kosofsky Sedgwick writes: '... the area over which homophobic prohibition maintains the most unyielding grasp is precollege education. What professor who cares for her students' survival, dignity, and thought can fail to be impressed and frightened by the unaccustomed, perhaps impossible responsibilities that devolve on college faculty as a result of the homophobia

uniformly enjoined on teachers throughout the primary and secondary levels of public school—where teachers are subject to being fired, not only for being visibly gay, but whatever their sexuality, for providing any intimation that homosexual desires, identities, cultures, adults, children, or adolescents have a right to expression or existence' (1990, 'Pedagogy,' 152).

10 See 'The Theatre of Implication' in *Canadian Theatre Review* 12 (Fall 1976), pp 34-41, in which Jackson writes: '... innuendo has been the chief means of conveying homosexual themes to the theatre audience. The reasons for this are rather obvious; they are based in large measure on the fundamental differences (structural and otherwise) between the novel and the play. The latter requires the intervention (or interference), of more people and demands greater finances, too, in order to reach its audience. The producer as we know him in the twentieth century, has had to approach the hitherto long-taboo subject of homosexuality with great caution in order to secure sound financial support. Backers, however, have not been the only group whose sensibilities have had to be appeased. The public, the majority of theatre-goers, have always insisted upon special protection from anything unpleasant. As many playwrights, directors, and producers have learned the hard way, one cannot always do on a stage what one could do without censure in a novel, the stage presentation packing a more immediate and less intellectual punch' (34).

11 The text of this play is published in *Canadian Theatre Review* 59 (Summer 1989), pp. 59-76.

Works Cited:

Boswell, John. *Christianity, Social Tolerance, and Homosexuality: Gay People in Western Europe from the Beginning of the Christian Era to the Fourteenth Century.* Chicago: University of Chicago Press, 1980.

Bronski, Michael. *Culture Clash: The Making of Gay Sensibility.* Boston: South End Press, 1984.

Chesebro, James W. *Gayspeak: Gay Male & Lesbian Communication.* New York: The Pilgrim Press, 1981.

de Lauretis, Teresa. 'Queer Theory: Lesbian and Gay Sexualities: An Introduction.' *differences* 3,2 (Summer 1991): iii-xviii.

Fuss, Diana. *Essentially Speaking: Feminism, Nature & Difference.* New York: Routledge, 1989.

———. 'Introduction.' *inside/out: Lesbian Theories, Gay Theories.* New York: Routledge, 1991: 1-10.

Gevisser, Mark. 'Gay Theater Today.' *Theater* XXI, 3 (Summer/Fall 1990): 46-51.

Goldie, Terry. 'Fresh Canons: The Native Canadian Example.' *English Studies in Canada* XVII, 4 (December 1991): 373-384.

Goodwin, Joseph P. *More Man than You'll Ever Be: Gay Folklore and Acculturation in Middle America.* Bloomington: Indiana University Press, 1989.

Holub, Robert C. *Reception Theory: A Critical Introduction.* London: Methuen, 1984.

Jackson, Graham. 'The Theatre of Implication.' *Canadian Theatre Review* 12 (Fall 1976): 34-41.

Martin, Robert K. *The Homosexual Tradition in American Poetry.* Austin: University of Texas Press, 1979.

———. 'Dryden's Dates: Reflections on Canons, Curricula, and Pedagogy.' *English Studies in Canada* XVII, 4 (December 1991): 385-399.

Patton, Cindy. *Inventing AIDS.* London: Routledge, 1990.

Sedgwick, Eve Kosofsky. *The Epistemology of the Closet.* Berkeley: University of California Press, 1990.

———. 'Pedagogy in the Context of an Anti-homophobic Project.' *South Atlantic Quarterly* 89, 1 (Winter 1990): 139-156.

Stambolian, George, ed. 'Introduction.' *Men on Men 2: Best New Gay Fiction.* New York: New American Library, 1988: 1-12.

Thompson, Mark. *Gay Spirit: Myth and Meaning.* New York: St. Martin's Press, 1987.

Wagner, Vit. 'Frank AIDS play challenges teens.' *Toronto Star* 3 April 1991: B3.

———. 'Gay Plays cut to the heart of unwanted relationships.' *Toronto Star* 26 April 1991: D14.

Weeks, Jeffrey. *Sexuality and its Discontents: Meanings, Myths & Modern Sexualities.* London: Routledge and Kegan Paul, 1985.

Yingling, Thomas. 'Sexual Preference/Cultural Reference: The Predicament of Gay Culture Studies.' *American Literary History* 3,1 (Spring 1991): 184-197.

Touch

A Play for Two
by David Demchuk

Touch was first produced by Buddies In Bad Times Theatre for the *Rhubarb!* festival in Toronto in February 1986 with the following cast:

GARY, Daniel MacIvor
KEN, Ron Jenkins

Producer: Sky Gilbert
Director: Audrey Butler
Production Manager: David Pond

For permission to perform the play please contact:

David Demchuk
c/o The Playwrights Union of Canada
54 Wolseley Street, Second Floor
Toronto, Canada
M5T 1A5

For Dennis, with love

Touch

House lights rise and stage lights fade out as music rises. KEN *and*
GARY *enter with bedding, a small lantern, and a plastic bag full
of magazines and books. They set the lantern down, prepare a
bed on the stage, remove their clothes, and climb in together.
Music fades, and a single light gently rises on the pair*

KEN [*thumbing through a magazine*] Any picture?

GARY Uh-huh. It's best, though, if there's more than one person.
[*answers* KEN*'s look*] Gives me more to work with. More to
imagine. You'll see what I mean.

KEN Mmn. [*pause*] Pretty grim stuff.

GARY Not all of it.

KEN Most of it.

GARY You'd think you'd never seen porn before.

KEN I've seen it. I don't much care for what I see.

GARY Well, there are other ways to see it, that's what I try to do.
Just humour me and find a picture, okay?

KEN [*shrugs. Pause*] Um ... okay. Found one. Two men. One is
on his knees, stripped to the waist. The other one is standing
beside him, pinching his nipple and jerking off into his mouth.
[*sighs*] The standing one is wearing a dirty undershirt, jeans
down around his ankles. Workboots. Looks like some kind of
factory or wood-shop. The standing guy has a wedding ring
on the hand he's jerking off with.

GARY That's it?

KEN Pretty well. A few empty beer cans, stuff like that. Some sawdust. They're both circumcised, if that helps at all.

GARY Nah. It might help if they weren't. I like uncircumcised men.

KEN You do?

GARY Okay, give me a sec. [*pause*] There are these two men, John and Michael.

KEN You name them.

GARY Yeah. It helps.

So. John and Michael. They're lovers, they've been together a long time. Seven, eight years. And they work together as carpenters.

KEN Eight years isn't so long.

Sorry.

GARY The one wearing the ring, Michael, he was married before he met John, still feels close to his former wife, but his past life doesn't worry John or make him feel threatened. In fact, they're both on good terms with her, they see her every once in a while.

KEN So they work together.

GARY I'm getting to it, I'm getting to it. Give me a minute.

KEN Just trying to help.

GARY So they work together. It's not hard for them, each can be at opposite ends of the shop from the other, doing different things, and except for whatever noise his lover makes he could feel like he was alone.

KEN Right.

GARY From time to time they work on larger things, they get along well, and neither one tries to be the boss. They're both good with their hands and between them they can solve any problem that comes up.

KEN So one day ...

GARY So one day they're working on something large—shelving, maybe a cabinet. Something. John starts being playful with

Michael, being physical ... the way they were when they first
started going out, you know, kind of silly.

KEN Why didn't I know you like uncircumcised men?

GARY What?

[*sighs*] Ken. Forget it, it's not a big deal. No big deal. Just,
you know, one of those things, an idiosyncrasy. A matter of
taste.

KEN Ha ha. Ha.

GARY There's no point in going on with all this if you're going to
take it all so seriously. My God, it's only sex. Everyone's a little
weird about sex. I am. God knows you are.

Do I go ahead or what?

KEN Go ahead. I'm listening.

GARY Where was I?

KEN John's being playful.

GARY Right. John's being playful.

So John's being playful. Michael doesn't pay any attention,
he just wants to get the job done. And sure enough, after a
few minutes, John seems to get the message, and he cools it.
Michael thinks for a moment that bad feelings might be
coming, but before he can say anything, John excuses himself
and goes into the washroom.

[*Pause*]

KEN Something wrong?

Gary, is something—

GARY Michael shrugs to himself, keeps doing what he's doing.

KEN What *is* he doing?

GARY I don't know. I don't know anything about carpentry.

KEN Oh.

GARY Anyway, he doesn't see John come out of the washroom,
only feels John's arm curve around him from behind, feels
John's hand slip into his shirt. This makes Michael drop

a bunch of nails he was holding. He looks down to where he dropped them and sees John's bare foot behind his, he sees John's bare leg ... he realizes that John is standing naked behind him. He turns around to say something, but John is already starting to kneel down, and when Michael turns around John grabs the front of Michael's jeans and undoes his fly.

Michael just sort of stands there, not knowing what to do. Anyone could walk in, anyone could pass by a window and see what's going on, but by this time John's going down on him, Michael doesn't want him to, but he doesn't want him to stop. He just keeps looking from window to window, listening for the click of the door, he imagines a customer coming in to check on something, or maybe his ex-wife. He can't stop, he thinks of the dinners they've had, all the nice conversations about ordinary things, all the time he spent staring at the new husband wondering what he looked like with his clothes off. Michael comes in John's mouth, and as he comes he's thinking ... about them ...

KEN That's it?

GARY That's it. End of story.

What do you think?

KEN I think ... I think it's sad.

I mean two people, in a relationship, they have such different perspectives on each other, on what they have together, you'd think that making love they'd ... *meet*, but even then each one of them is still ... you know ... alone ...

Is that what it's always like? For everyone?

GARY It's just a fantasy. Just a story.

KEN Is this what you'd think of, then, seeing this picture in this magazine?

GARY Probably. Maybe not so much like a story with a beginning and an ending, but otherwise it's kind of what would run through my head.

KEN Mmn.

GARY What else did you think?

KEN Well, you made them seem like real people, like lovers ... and it was sexy, I guess ...

GARY You guess?

KEN But ... I don't know, the men you were talking about seemed as trapped as the ones in the picture.

GARY Trapped?

KEN Yeah, I don't know how to explain it better. I'll have to think about it.

It is only the first one. We can try another.

GARY Yeah, maybe it was just the way I told it.

KEN [*thumbs through another magazine, then stops*] Gary?

GARY Yeah?

KEN Why did you stop telling the story when you did? When John went into the washroom?

GARY I don't know, I guess I thought it sounded like us, a bit. I was waiting for you to say something.

KEN Oh. I didn't notice.

Anyway, this one has two guys who are brothers. One's about thirty, the other is probably just over eighteen but he looks younger. They have the same colour eyes and hair, similar faces. The older one is holding the other one down on the bed and is fucking him. There's an open porn magazine near the younger one's head. It probably belongs to the older brother and was being read by the younger one when the older one walked in and jumped him.

GARY How do you figure all that? How do you even know they're brothers?

KEN [*shrugs*] I saw the video. Anyway, that's the picture.

GARY Where did you see the video?

KEN Never mind where. You've got the picture, do something with it.

GARY That's not the only picture I've got. Where did you see the video?

KEN Paul's. They revised his job description and gave him a raise, so he bought himself a VCR and ordered a few movies.

GARY When?

KEN Months ago, two, maybe three months ago.

GARY Where was I?

KEN God, do *I* know? Am I supposed to remember? You were out of town somewhere, I think, probably visiting your mother.

GARY Well, thanks for telling me all about it as soon as I got back.

KEN Like you would have cared. [*sighs*] Well, obviously you do and I didn't think you would. I'm sorry.

   I said sorry.

GARY I thought you didn't like porn. Or is it only my porn you don't like.

KEN Gary, I didn't buy the VCR or the movies, and I didn't ask him to play them for me. I *was* a bit curious, but …

GARY But what?

KEN But it was a waste of time because they were boring.

GARY Oh.

   What we're doing tonight, is this boring?

KEN Which, looking at your magazines, or fighting about what I do when you're out of town?

GARY I accept your apology.

KEN Can we get on with this?

GARY Sure.

   Sure, the picture—

KEN Brothers.

GARY Right. Give me a sec.

KEN All the time you want. I have to be at work in, what, four hours?

GARY Oh, calm down. I think I've got it.

The younger one's name is Steve.

KEN It was John in the video.

Sorry. Steve's fine. Whatever you like.

GARY The younger one's name ... is John. The older one ...

KEN Jim.

GARY Anything else I should know?

KEN They're circumcised.

GARY Right.

Anything else?

KEN I don't think so.

GARY Good.

KEN If I think of something, I'll tell you.

GARY No doubt. Now. Jim, the older brother, he came out to his parents when he was eighteen. John was only four or five, too young to know what was going on. Finally, Jim moved out and he stopped speaking to his parents for several years. When he and his parents did start talking again, he began to visit, though not very often. When he did visit, his parents never let him be alone with his brother, only rarely let him hold or play with him.

KEN Must've been hard on them both.

GARY Harder on Jim, I think. Being shut out of the family, and then when some kind of peace is made, you know, they still don't trust you.

KEN Watching every move you make.

GARY Yeah. Now John, he daydreamed about his older brother during all of this, made him into kind of an imaginary close friend. Gradually, John's own homosexuality began to surface in crushes on teachers, on other boys in school. And on the brother he barely knew.

KEN We're still nowhere near the picture.

GARY Right. Well.

When John turns fifteen, Jim calls him and invites him to his apartment, he hasn't seen John for a while and he wants to talk about something. John thinks about it for a while, finally decides to go see him. Takes him an hour to get to this house on the other side of the city, Jim rents the top two floors, a nice place. He offers John a beer, John hesitates before he accepts.

KEN That's nice. The thing about the beer, it's a nice touch.

GARY You like that? Maybe I should be a writer.

KEN Not that nice a touch.

GARY Anyway, Jim is just about to tell John why he asked him to come, when the guy who lives downstairs knocks and asks Jim to help move a piano from one room to another, a ten-minute job. While Jim is gone, John explores the apartment. He goes into the bedroom, sees beside the bed a pile of magazines, a bottle of hand cream lying across them. He looks through them, finds page after page of men having sex with other men, something he's imagined but never seen before. Sure that he'll hear his brother return, he undoes his pants, squeezes some of the hand cream onto himself, and begins to masturbate. He looks at the pictures, imagines his friends, imagines teachers, strangers, finally himself and his brother. He hears the door open downstairs and he doesn't stop, he hears his brother coming up the stairs, hears him pass the bedroom door, then his footsteps halting, his voice calling out, the door opening. John closes his eyes, holds in his breath, he doesn't stop, he moans as he starts to come, he doesn't stop doesn't open his eyes doesn't open until he feels the warmth of his brother over and near him, until he feels his brother's hair brush by his cheek, his chest, he feels his brother's mouth around him, pulling, pulling. John opens his eyes and looks down at his brother, Jim, looking up at him.

KEN And Jim spits in John's eye because he has a mouth full of hand cream.

GARY Maybe you should be the writer.

KEN I don't think so.

GARY Well. Was that one any better?

KEN Well. No, not really. Not for me, anyway.

GARY Why not?

KEN It doesn't matter.

GARY Come on. At least say that it was better than the video.

KEN Gary, this is what the video was like. Two brothers are sitting around, telling each other about who they've slept with for the past few months. After five or six flashbacks, the older one goes to the bathroom, the younger goes to the bedroom, starts jerking off over a magazine, the older one goes in and fucks him. The end. So. I guess your version was better than the video, but I still don't see why you use porn if you can use your imagination instead.

GARY Because even though I don't like the images, they excite me. It excites me to see pictures of naked men, or of men having sex, especially if I find the men attractive.

KEN But your fantasies are still about gay men hurting each other or being hurt by other people. Or running scared. You sidestepped the violence, but not the message. Not completely. That's not changing the image, it's just rearranging it for your own tastes.

GARY You're the one who wants porn rearranged to suit your tastes. You're threatened by these magazines, that's what it is. You think that sex between us should be enough, well, sometimes it's not.

KEN [grabs a magazine. Opens it] Some naked kid, he's handcuffed to a cot in a jail cell, he's being fucked in the ass by a cop in full uniform and helmet, the only flesh the cop shows apart from the area around his sunglasses is the foot or so sticking out of his pants.

[thumbs through another] A soldier—a black soldier, mind

you—his wrists are tied together, he hangs from a hook in the ceiling of a stone room while two white military men beat him, shave his body, pierce his nipples. Each one rapes him while the other watches, jerking off. I'm not threatened by these, I'm insulted by them. I don't know why you need them, I couldn't believe it when you brought them with you when we first moved in together. Every once in a while a new one shows up on top of the pile, I thumb through it and I ask myself why. But I don't ask you. And I don't throw them out, though I think about it more and more.

GARY Well fine. We'll throw them out. [*begins stuffing magazines back into the bag*] Come on, let's throw them out and go to sleep, and tomorrow everything will be back to normal again.

What do you want from me? Do you want me to tell you I'm fucked up? Fine. I'm fucked up. Not a lot, I don't act on any of my fantasies. No, I just think about these things for twenty minutes or so every couple of days, I come, I zip my pants up, things are swell. Maybe I don't think the best of myself. It doesn't mean I'm a monster.

KEN What do you think about when we're making love?

Do you think about me? Or do you think about these?

GARY [*long pause*] Right. We won't throw them out, we'll burn them. I'll get the wok out of the kitchen, we'll burn them. Porno dim sum.

Better yet, I'll stand in the wok and set fire to myself while I watch you pack your things and leave me. [*sighs*] There is no God, is there?

KEN If I was going to leave you over this shit, I would've left a long time ago. I'm not going to leave you, at least I don't think I am. I just want to know. We have to talk about it.

GARY Fine. Fine. When I'm—

Oh, God. I don't know how to—

KEN Just talk.

Daniel MacIvor (**GARY**) and Ron Jenkins (**KEN**)
Photographer: Donna Marchand

GARY Well ...

Well, I guess it mostly has to do with how I see myself, how I feel about myself being gay ... We're all raised to hate and be afraid of gays, and then things have to change when we understand we're gay ourselves, but, I don't know, I guess a lot of what I was raised with has really stuck. I've gone out of my way to have a lot of bad experiences, I guess because I never believed I deserved better. One time, my best friend's dad, in his basement ... no one home ... I remember him on top of me and me thinking, There's nothing wrong with him, he's Lyle's dad. There's nothing wrong with him, there's something wrong with me. I've felt it there for years, and this is what it will be for me, always. And so there's kind of this split, inside of me, between my mind and my body, and ...

... and when we make love, when you touch me, there's some part of me where it doesn't happen, where the touch isn't happening ... and then it's one of two things.

The first is that I stop thinking about my own feelings, and I turn all my attention to you, to making you feel good ...

The second thing is for me to fantasize, sometimes about stuff in here, sometimes about other things ...

... Lyle's dad ... other things ...

Other times I fantasize about you with other men, or my ex-lovers having sex with other men, or each other ...

I have to hurt myself, a little, to feel anything at all.

So ... what now?

KEN I don't know.

GARY Does it make sense?

KEN Kind of. I guess. I have to think about it more.

GARY I shouldn't have brought these out, I shouldn't have tried to make you understand. I shouldn't have said anything.

I should've lied.

KEN No, Gary ...

GARY We're the image, you and I. We're the picture.

[*sarcastic*] Two men in bed, two men who love each other, who love each other, who know each other so well ... I know you but I've never ... felt you ...

I've always been alone in here, with you so far away beside me, trying to reach ...

What's wrong with this picture ... what's wrong ...

KEN Nothing ... [*responds to* GARY*'s hostile look*] *Fine.*

Not nothing. But it's stuff we can work on ... talk about ...
We can make it through this.

GARY [*deep sigh*] Two men, their names are Ken and Gary.
They're lovers, they've been together for just over a year.
And they love each other ... they ...

KEN ... they touch ...

[*End*]

Beuys Buoys Boys

A Monologue
by Ken Garnhum

Beuys Buoys Boys was first produced by Tarragon Theatre in Toronto in January 1989.

Performer and Designer: Ken Garnhum
Director: Andy McKim
Lighting Designer: Kevin Lamotte
Stage Manager: Marta Stothers

It was remounted for the duMaurier World Stage Festival in Toronto in June 1990.

Performer and Designer: Ken Garnhum
Director: Andy McKim
Lighting Designer: Kevin Lamotte
Stage Manager: Allan Clements

For permission to perform the play please contact:

Ken Garnhum
c/o Tarragon Theatre
30 Bridgman Avenue
Toronto, Canada
M5R 1X3

Notes on Staging:

Beuys Buoys Boys does not require a realistic setting but it does require a visual one; objects and images should play an important role. The performance space is a neutral space—a 'found' space that has been claimed, or is in the process of being claimed, by the performer. When the performer leaves the space at the end of the piece, he leaves it unaltered, with the singular exception of the monument. The erection of this monument is the central action of *Beuys Buoys Boys;* it is the performer's ultimate gesture; it is the mark he leaves behind. There is an attempt in the body of the text to describe the monument and the process of building/assembling it. Directors and designers should feel free to invent, keeping in mind that the monument should, when it is completed, suggest a buoy on the open sea, and that this resemblance to a buoy should be a visual surprise near the end of the performance. This idea of a visual surprise is an important one. When the text notes say that something 'appears,' the appearance should be unexpected, or even—occasionally—magical. The act of drawing is essential to *Beuys Buoys Boys*, as is the appearance of projected images to support and enhance particular passages of the spoken text. Placement of drawing and slide sequences are indicated in the text, but are described in such a way as to leave much room for invention. Lighting and sound should also play their part in creating a theatrical atmosphere. But the text, for the most part, leaves it to individual directors and designers to decide where these important tools can best be used.

This script is dedicated to the innocent, dead of AIDS.

Beuys Buoys Boys

It is dark. The performer enters with a hand-held light and delivers the Prologue

PERFORMER Late at night, in the dead of winter, the road would look so black—flanked, as it was, by the high, white banks of snow. The patches of ice on the road would look blacker still, black on black. The telephone wires hummed loud in the cold air, and every once in a while the air itself would seem to crack. And a million stars.

[*Stars appear*]

I would be walking home from babysitting at the MacLeans', a couple that actually stayed up late and went to town on a Saturday night. Everyone else was asleep: the Gays, the Judsons, the Wetherbys, the Garnhums, even the goddamn Jenkinses, all asleep.

But then I would think, maybe they're not asleep, maybe they're all dead—yeah, dead—poisoned quietly and painlessly in their sleep by some insidious gas, and now all of the houses are uninhabitable, but I also instinctively know that I have ten minutes in which to enter the houses and collect what I will need to survive. My mind immediately begins to construct a list. Quilts! I decide to collect as many quilts as possible so that I can build a yurt in the back field, just like the Mongolians in the *National Geographic* at the MacLeans'. A quilt tent.

I think about this just about every Saturday night for a whole winter.

[*Hand-held light out. Stars fade to black slowly during the following voice-over, which is spoken, à la Joseph Beuys, with a German accent*]

'I was completely buried in the snow. That's how the Tartars found me days later. I remember voices saying "voda" (water), then the felt of their tents, and the dense pungent smell of cheese, fat and milk. They covered my body in fat, to help regenerate warmth, and wrapped it in felt as an insulator to keep the warmth in.'

[*End of the* Prologue. *Lights up on the performer, who is wearing a Beuysian grey-felt hat and felt boots. He is pacing, laying claim to the performance space. He speaks, as he will more or less throughout the performance, directly to the audience*]

What a day—what a heavenly day! This is not mere rhetoric—I really mean it. Today is a happy day, because today is the day that I get to put it all together. You see, a while back I got this incredibly strong urge to build. Just that—an urge to build—I had no idea what it was that I was going to build; I just knew that I had to build something, period! And I thought, boy, this is just a little abstract. I mean, usually I get these burning ideas and I have to go about deciding how best to manifest the ideas, but this was a different kettle of fish. I tried to ignore the urge, but it was strong; it stuck with me, and so I began to concentrate on it. I tried to find the idea behind the urge and I was surprised that my mind kept coming back to monuments. *Monuments*—this seemed strange indeed, because I've always thought that most monuments are a big wank; and there are too damn many of them; and they have very little to do with what I think public art should be about.

Most public monuments are diversionary at best—they divert our attention away from the present to the past; and they are demanding—they demand reverence for gods, or heroes, or rulers who often deserve much less. Let's face it—most public monuments are just big, ugly, expensive hulks of metal, paid for with public money, to celebrate wars, and kings, and politicians who acted against the public interest.

Monuments are tricky bloody things, too. They often derive their power with sheer scale. A bronze figure of some wanker the same size as me is nothing compared to one forty, or fifty, or sixty feet high.

[*First slide in a sequence of slides of monuments—some literal, some figurative—appears at this point. It depicts a huge bronze figure*]

Suddenly, we are so diminished that the merely huge becomes powerful. But, I discovered, something doesn't have to look like this [*refers to slide*] to be a monument. Any memorial,

[*Slide of tombstone*]

a tombstone, for example, is a monument. A monument can be a mere indication, something that serves to identify or mark,

[*Slide of a roadside granite marker or a Beuys sculpture*]

something that gives a warning, a portent.

[*Slide of buoy on the ocean*]

There are many monuments to industry,

[*Slide of industrial smokestack*]

and many monuments to capitalism.

[*Slide of a bank skyscraper*]

Monuments can be extremely ugly,

[*Slide of* Gumby Goes to Heaven, *a monument on University Avenue in Toronto*]

or profoundly beautiful,

[*Slide of the War Memorial in Ottawa*]

in spite of, or occasionally because of what they commemorate.

[*Additional slides chosen by the performer*]

Anything, that by its survival, commemorates a person or action or time, is a monument. We are monuments; each of us is a monument to those whom we have lost, because we are the enduring evidence.

[*End of slide sequence. Beginning of a drawing sequence. Throughout the next section of the text the performer will draw with white and coloured chalk on a chalkboard. There could be chalkboards on easels, or part of the set or theatre wall could be a big chalkboard. The performer draws to illustrate his text as he speaks*]

In addition to scale, a monument can derive power from its situation, its site. [*drawing*] The site of a classical monument, for example, was always carefully chosen or constructed: in the centre of a square; at the end of a long, tree-lined avenue; or in front of a suitable building, almost as if the building were put there solely to be a backdrop for the monument. The site of a monument is its focal point—it is a theatrical space—it is a trick. The first time I found myself in New York City on my own I headed right for the Guggenheim Museum. [*drawing*] I'd seen photographs of it, and I found its spiralling architecture irresistible, like a kid with a Slinky. When I arrived outside of the museum I almost expected to be sucked up inside it from the street. Ironically, what I hadn't given much thought to at all was Art—what was inside this particular monument to Art. I didn't have a clue as to what was being exhibited at the time—and so it was that I had my first encounter with the work of the great German artist Joseph Beuys.

I didn't know a whole helluva lot about Joseph Beuys at this time—just the art-world hype, really. I mean, I knew that he was a pretty interesting guy—a man who believed that one could mix history, and science, and politics, and mysticism together to make art. I knew that Beuys was the man who made sculptures—social sculpture—out of fat and felt. And I knew that because of these and other things about Joseph Beuys and his work, he was regarded by half of the art world as a nut and a charlatan, while the other half revered him as a kind of benevolent *Art God*.

Anyway—the Guggenheim show turned out to be his first American retrospective—so there was lots of fat, piles of felt, and many delicate marks on paper. However, I remember vividly one particular work. It was a sculptural piece called *The Pack:* a Volkswagen van stood, open-ended, at the top of the incredible spiral which is the Guggenheim; pouring out the back of this van, and seemingly racing down the slope, were twenty identical wooden sleds; [*drawing*] packed on the back of each sled was a tight roll of felt, a serious chunk of fat, and a large, powerful flashlight. They seemed alive, these sleds, and absolutely determined. One sensed that there was a mission here, and that it was desperate. Not only that, but there seemed also to be a warning in this sculpture, and one felt that this warning was real and important because it was based on some-thing real: it was based on Joseph Beuys' personal history.

[*The voice-over of Beuys' words at the end of the* Prologue *is repeated here*]

'I was completely buried in the snow. That's how the Tartars found me days later. I remember voices saying "voda" (water), then the felt of their tents, and the dense pungent smell of cheese, fat and milk. They covered my body in fat, to help regenerate warmth, and wrapped it in felt as an insulator to keep the warmth in.'

[*End of first drawing sequence. A chair suggesting a tree appears*]

In 1961, Joseph Beuys was appointed to the Professorial Chair of Monumental Sculpture, at the Dusseldorf Academy of Art. [*the performer sits*] The early sixties was a time when, conceptually speaking, some pretty heady ideas were bouncing around the art world. To oversimplify—it was a time when many artists decided that the idea for a work of art was more important than the artwork itself—that 'process' would take precedence over 'product.'

[*Slide sequence of Beuys' sculpture*]

Joseph Beuys was always making ideas manifest. Joseph Beuys was always making monuments. In performing his 'Actions,' even just in speaking, he created monuments. Sometimes he memorialized ideas themselves; often he memorialized himself and his experiences; but always his works are invested with a relatedness to an idea, or an experience, or a memory, conscious or unconscious, that is transmitted to us as a feeling. We feel the work; and even when the object of his memorializing remains a mystery to us, we feel the mystery. And more than that, we feel the energy inherent in the mystery, and if we cannot feel the energy inherent in a work of art, then why bother?! Words won't help—all of the words, all of the explanations in the world, will not make it meaningful for us.

Words! Boy—there are so many words about Joseph Beuys,

and many of them came from Beuys himself. Like many great artists, like Brecht, for example, Beuys often said far too much about his work; but words are important, and explanations are irresistible. Joseph Beuys believed that his art could be explained, and should be explained, yet he constantly confronted us, his audience, with works of art whose greatest strength is their mystery. This is what we must confront first, before any words, before intellectualizing.

[*End of slide sequence of Beuys' sculptures*]

So—when I said that this is a happy day because it is the day that I get to put it all together—this is what I meant. I'm building a monument. I've collected and shaped all the pieces, and they are even paid for. It seems that I am forever working at one thing to pay for the materials to create another thing. I remember I had this job once ... [*the performer sits. Goes off on a tangent*] right after college. I was the assistant display artist in a big department store in Charlottetown, Prince Edward Island. The store was called Holman's of P.E.I. ... I did the windows, dressing ancient mannequins which had an average of 2.5 fingers each hand, and wigs like plastic helmets; I made a lot of polyester rosettes in Fabricland, a lot of Styrofoam tin soldiers for Toyland; *and* I was in charge of Santa Claus—I was truly Santa's helper. From the twelfth of November until the twenty-fourth of December, I brushed the beard, stocked the candy canes, and made copious cups of tea for Mr. MacLean. That was Santa's real name—Mr. MacLean. I was actually quite lucky; previous Santas had been a series of drunks from the hardware department, but my Santa was a piece of cake, a real doll, no trouble at all. No trouble that is, until the day of the 'May Your Every Christmas Wish Come True 20% Off Everything In The Store Except Tobacco And Appliances Sale'—one of those horrible ten-'til-midnight-every-lunatic-in-the-province-comes-out-to-shop sales, and Santa and I were expected to be in a dozen different places at the same time, all day long. So, at about four in the afternoon, I noticed that the seventy-five-year-old Mr. MacLean was looking a little the worse for wear, and so I insisted he come up to my fourth-floor, cubby-hole office so that I could make him a nice cup of English Breakfast. I made him sit in my chair, which was the only approximately comfortable one in the room, I gave him a stack of lingerie sales flyers to put his feet up on, and I handed him his tea. His prompt response was to fall off my chair and die, right there at my astonished feet, beard askew, red hat rolling, rolling away. And to this day, whenever anyone mourns the figurative death of Santa Claus in their childhood, I have very little sympathy. After all, I have experienced the literal one.

But Holman's was just one of two experiences in retail hell. The second was my stint at a Dominion Playworld in a mall in Stoney Creek, Ontario. I know that doesn't sound too hellish—so let me put it this way—I worked in the doll department of a toy store in a busy, suburban mall at Christmastime the year that the Barbie camper came out. We had waiting lists, we had all-female fist-fights, we had attempted bribery, it was a nightmare. I learned my first truly nasty lesson about human nature and consumerism, but I learned something of even more importance—I learned that there is something absolutely irresistible about an accessory for a Barbie doll. This special knowledge stayed with me all these years, resulting in the project I am about to unveil, a project that I hope will pay for many materials in the years to come ... Barbie's Beckett!

[Barbie's Beckett *is a Barbie-size stage-set on which a Barbie doll performs scenes from Samuel Beckett plays. In this scene, she is discovered lounging under a leafless tree in a comfortable recliner, watching television. She is dressed as Barbie would dress if she were asked to play Vladmir in* Waiting for Godot. *This miniature set appears, disappears, and reappears several times, as noted, throughout* Beuys Buoys Boys]

See ... she's 'waiting for Godot.' 'Was I sleeping, while the others suffered? Am I sleeping now? Tomorrow, when I wake, or think I do, what shall I say of today?'

So ... what do you think? Pretty catchy, eh! You'll notice that while the tree is distinctly Beckettian, the total setting is pure Barbie. This is just the prototype, but I hope to go into full production soon. I had some difficulty with the costume, I'm not much of a tailor, and this really crazy thing happened. I got fed up and I was finally sewing Barb right into her costume, and, well, I accidentally stuck a pin into her, and the next morning I got up and read in the paper that Miss Canada had collapsed the night before. So I went right out and bought Barbie's dark-haired companion, Midge, and stuck a few pins in her, but Mila Mulroney is still walking around. Well, I guess we should let her wait in peace.

[Barbie's Beckett *disappears*]

[*The performer refers to the jumble of chalkboard drawings he has made*]

Boy—if someone else waltzed in here right now, they'd have an interesting time deciphering all of this, wouldn't they? Whole blackboards on easels, with Joseph Beuys' marks on them, have been preserved and marketed by art dealers. Beuys was highly regarded as a teacher, and he rarely spoke to groups or students without drawing, writing, or otherwise making marks on a blackboard. Like his view of art in general, Beuys' view of drawing, of just what a drawing is, was quite broad. He defined a drawing as any kind of a notation, whether it reproduces a traditional figure, or whether it merely consists of a verbal explanation, or an idea. I like this definition, because the way we make a mark, our gesture, is of fundamental importance to drawing.

[*Beginning of another sequence of drawing to illustrate the spoken text*]

How we each write is a personal gesture, and that is why some people believe that they can read a personality by analysing handwriting. In a drawing, the object or idea drawn is important, of course, [*drawing*] but 'how' it is drawn, the quality of the line, the gesture, is what invests the drawing with its meaning. For example, [*drawing*] if I were to draw a skull ... it would be very different from a skull drawn by Georgia O'Keefe ... I can't pretend to represent O'Keefe drawing accurately, although I do find that in attempting to reproduce her style, no matter what the subject, be it flower or skull, if you begin with that old vulva, you will get there eventually ... or ... if we were lucky enough to have had Joseph Beuys draw a skull for us [*still drawing*] ... anyway, what I am trying to show is that the quality of the lines, even the approach to the chalkboard, is very different in each of these examples. The lines in a Beuys drawing are extremely delicate, somewhat tentative, though not insecure, and always mysterious. Actually, if we had asked Joseph Beuys to draw a skull for us, he might have reacted by trowelling some fat into a corner—you never know.

Leaving behind a line is leaving behind a noticeable trace of an impulse.

[*End of drawing sequence*]

Beuys left many such traces. Beuys was a great teacher because of his need to 'show' ideas.

Well ... I should get to work. Oh—let's check on Barbie first, shall we?

[Barbie's Beckett *reappears*]

Yep, she's still waiting.

[Barbie's Beckett *disappears*]

[*The performer exits and quickly reappears pulling a red cart. This cart contains the monument—wooden sections that, when assembled, form a brightly-coloured obelisk which will eventually be topped with a light-emitting pyramid. The entire obelisk will then be placed on the inverted cart, which becomes the base of the monument. The top of the cart should be raked, so that when the cart has been inverted the whole monument sits at a jaunty angle, as if it were a buoy on the sea*]

'You captains tell the guns to slacken
And give the infanteers a break;
It's Mother Courage with her wagon
Full of the finest boots they make ...'

Just kidding, it's me!

[*Throughout the next scene, the performer sorts his tools and materials from the cart, in preparation for actual assembly*]

I made a monument once before, a long time ago. It was an angel on wheels. Like many kids, my friends and I used to have funerals for the variety of dead creatures that our community produced, from, say, water beetles, on a slow day, right up to the squirrels and occasional cats that the friggin' Jenkins boys would kill with their BB guns. I saved boxes, any and all boxes, from match boxes to boot-boxes, so that in the event of a death, I would solemnly usher the bereaved into my room to pick out a suitable coffin, which my partner, Hazel Judson, and I would then decorate. After this, we would have an elaborate funeral procession; we'd go up the Pownal Road, and then turn down the Shore Road, proceeding to our cemetery beside Reanney Gay's fishing shack on the beach. Our processions got more and more grand, until one day we decided that we needed a new hearse—Hazel's wagon just wasn't good enough. So ... I built this angel on wheels, I built her with these flat, outstretched arms that held the coffin up for all the world to see. In spite of even the angel, we remained unsatisfied; we had become obsessed with our funerals. Then, Hazel came to me, all excited because she had read in the *National Geographic* that the early Egyptians had buried valuables with their dead because they believed that the dead would need their earthly goods in the next world. Well—we thought this was pretty fabulous—so, from then on, whenever we had a big funeral coming up, Hazel and I would go up the road to Horne's Store, and we would buy candy necklaces and surprise packages, and we'd put all the best stuff in with the corpse. And old Mrs. Horne—she was just great. She'd see us coming a mile away, and we'd walk in, and she'd get this really long look on her face, and say, 'Oh dear, it's not another death, is it? It's been a terrible hard week for you two, now hasn't it? You must accept our deepest condolences,' and great shit like that. We just loved her for it.

Before the end of the summer, though, the entire funeral enterprise came crashing to an end when it was discovered that Dilly Cannon was digging up the graves and eating all the candy. Poor Dilly—it's a wonder she didn't die. Now—a child psychologist might say all that ritual interaction with dead creatures was natural, a necessary introduction to death ... but

I'm here to tell you that burying a rat that Tommy Jenkins killed with a shovel in George Lawton's potato barn was no help at all when it came to people.

[*The performer sits in his tree-chair to tell the following story*]

My mother told me that Keith MacKenzie was dead. Keith was a foster kid and, as a result, he was tormented by every other kid his age in the community, and by some old enough to know better. My quiet brother David was an exception. Keith and David were best friends, and on the rare occasions that Keith got off the farm, he would end up hanging around our place. He almost worshipped our mother, and I think that was because she treated him exactly the same way as she treated every other kid we brought home; which is to say, she teased the 'bejesus' out of him, and every once in a while she'd wrestle him to the floor and kiss him on the neck.

At that time, I certainly thought that I was far too sophisticated to pay much attention to my little brother's buddies, but I did treat Keith with a respect that he got precious little of. When she told me, she spoke very quietly, and she said that when the tractor flipped over he was most likely killed instantly. I was quiet myself for a long time, but when I started to cry, I couldn't stop. I can remember my mother sitting beside me on my bed with her arm around my shoulder, saying over and over, 'It's alright Kenny, it's alright. You were always really nice to Keith; it's all those Mutch kids and Doyle kids who should feel bad, not you.' Then my father—Mr. Patience—he yells from the kitchen that if I don't stop my goddamn crying soon, they'll have to take me to town for a needle, but I couldn't stop.

[*Slide with the word* Fear *appears*]

[*Throughout the next scene, the performer tries to re-create, at least in spirit, the Beuysian Action that he is describing, using whatever objects and set pieces are at hand. Among these objects are the performer's Beuysian hat and a large piece of felt. The performer howls like a coyote to start the scene]*

A coyote. For the First Nations of North America, the coyote was one of the mightiest of all deities. The coyote could change its state from the physical to the spiritual, and vice versa, at will. The coyote was respected and venerated because of its ingenuity and its adaptability. Upon arrival, however, the white man decided that the coyote was actually low, cunning and untrustworthy—talk about the pot calling the kettle black. Anyway, all of a sudden the coyote was despised and persecuted.

The coyote was of great interest to Joseph Beuys, partly because of his overall interest in the animal world, specifically the connections between the natural world and the world of the spirit, but also because he saw embodied in the coyote what he called 'a psychological trauma point of the United States,'—and, that is to say—America's trauma with its indigenous peoples.

So—in 1976, when Joseph Beuys was scheduled to exhibit at the Rene Bloch Gallery in New York City, he had himself picked up at the airport, immediately wrapped in felt, and then driven at high speed, in the back of an ambulance, directly to the gallery, where he quickly incarcerated himself in an exhibition space with more felt, a walking-stick, a flashlight and other small items, fifty copies of that day's *Wall Street Journal* (which were changed daily throughout the exhibition), *and* a live coyote. Mr. Beuys and the Coyote lived together in this room for three days, and during this time Mr. Beuys performed a number of repeated ritual actions. At any given moment he might ring a little triangle that he wore around his neck and then wait for the coyote's response. There are many photographs documenting this event; photographs of a tall figure shrouded in grey felt, with a long walking-stick projecting upwards, like some great shepherd, and a wild dog with his teeth in the felt, pulling and pulling at the man; the epitome of the tension between nature and culture.

[*The performer completes his Action*]

Now—all this stuff about trauma points and ritual observation is interesting, *but* like Samuel Beckett's *Waiting for Godot,* what *Coyote* is really about is isolation. Isolation and communication, the possibilities and the impossibilities of communication.

[*The performer delivers the next section of the text wrapped in felt*]

I saw another Beuys installation at the Anthony D'Offay Gallery in London. It was called *Felt Room,* and as you might surmise from the title, it was indeed a room that was completely enveloped in felt; but not just felt hanging from the walls—great whacking rolls of felt banked together on all the walls and the ceiling—and, in the centre of the room—a grand piano also swathed in felt—rendered unplayable, mute.

[*The performer emerges from his felt*]

Joseph Beuys said of the *Felt Room* that 'everything is taken away which is genuinely communicative ... like Beckett's plays ... everything is isolated, and knocking on the walls has no resonance.'

Speaking of *Godot,* shall we see if Barbie is still waiting?

[*Barbie's stage reappears, but now Barbie is in a scene from Beckett's* Happy Days. *She is buried up to her waist in sand, her hair is elaborately curled, and she has make-up and magazines scattered around her*]

Oh wow, now it really is a happy day! Another heavenly day.
'Days perhaps when you hear nothing … But days too when
you answer … So that I may say at all times, even when you do
not answer and perhaps hear nothing, something of this is
being heard, I am not merely talking to myself … a thing I
could never bear to do …' This must be the first act of *Happy
Days* since Barbie, I mean Winnie, is only buried to her waist.
In the second act she is buried to her neck, which is why we
decided that 'hair' is so important to Barbie's *Happy Days*. In
fact, it comes with a total of four wigs—this Dolly Parton one,
as well as an Ali McGraw, a Doris Day, and a Kathleen
Turner—in other words, one for each actor that Barbie and
I would just love to see buried up to her neck in dirt.

[Barbie's Beckett *disappears. A microwave oven appears*]

Breaktime!

[*The performer opens the oven and extracts a metal lunch-pail. He
opens the lunch-pail and takes out a mug of coffee which he places
back in the oven to heat up. He waits*]

I love to cook. When I was a kid I used to watch Madame
Benoit cooking on the CBC; I loved everything that woman
did and said. I loved her Tenderflake commercials, remember:
'I love dat wurd—Tenderflake. To me it say two ting, it say
"tender," and it say "flaky."'

[*Coffee is hot. The performer sits near the audience, eating rice-
cakes from the lunch-pail, sipping coffee, and talking*]

I actually saw her cooking, live, once; it was in a mall in
Charlottetown. I was just walking through, and there she was,
bigger than life, and in the middle of preparing a cream of
turnip. As I sat down, she was saying: 'In making de cream of
turneep, you can use de budder, because de turneep and de

Ken Garnhum in *Beuys Buoys Boys*
Photographer: Michael Cooper

budder, dey are friend, *but*, I use de cream because de turneep
and de cream, dey are lovers.' How could you not love a
woman who spoke like that?! She even made microwaves seem
somehow passionate, spiritual. She was once asked what she
would say to people who only use their microwaves to heat
coffee and to make popcorn, and she replied: 'I would tell dem
dat I will say tree Hail Mary for dem every night.' You may not
believe that I can cook since all I have are these, [*referring to the
rice-cakes*] but they were the only thing I thought I could eat in
front of people without feeling guilty. [*eats, obviously without
enjoyment*] I've always thought that there is a correlation
between cooking and drawing. I mean, I spoke earlier about
how artists must have a particular gesture with which they

invest their works with meaning; well, I think that the same goes for good cooks as well. Madame Benoit certainly had a gesture that shaped her works; there is that trace of the cook's impulse in any good food. I even think I know what Madame Benoit's gesture was. In her last interview before her death, she interrupted the CBC radio interviewer mid-question, and she said: 'Non—what I really want to talk about is love.' [*performer pauses. Eating, thinking*]

Anyone been having any housing problems lately? 'Does Rose Kennedy have a black dress'—right? In my ten or so years here, I have managed to develop a pretty impressive paranoia about housing. Every renter has at least one good horror story; I have several myself, but even my own stories seem minuscule when viewed in the larger picture. Not long ago, I was walking down the Rosedale Valley Road and I had this uncomfortable feeling that I was being followed. Eventually I became sure that I was, so I slowed down—real bright, eh—thinking the person might pass me. But he slowed down, too. This made me very nervous, so I took off like a bat out of hell. When I finally stopped and turned around, no one was there, not a trace. That was when I realized that whoever had been behind me lived there, in the ravine, and that he simply did not want me to see where; the privacy of homelessness. My mind went immediately back to a time in my childhood when I used to drag cardboard and boards into the woods and build forts, often with Peter Worth, but that's another story, and anyway, then I would beg my mother to let me sleep out there, but she never would. And now—now I'm afraid that I will end up doing just that after all.

[*End of the break. The performer sits in his tree-chair*]

When my Aunt Muriel died, we had quite a time of it. It all began at the funeral with poor Maureen—Maureen—she was

Aunt Muriel's daughter, my father's first cousin. The trouble really started because of that perverse custom many funeral homes have of ceremoniously closing the lid of the coffin just moments before the actual funeral service begins. You see, at that point, they always ask if any member of the immediate family would like to say a final goodbye to the dearly departed, as it were, and of course Maureen says yes. My father and I stood at opposite ends of the casket, kind of like sentinels, and so we were the ones who had to deal with it. Maureen drags herself up that aisle as if she would surely be the next one to depart this earthly toil, and when she got to the coffin she grabbed a hold of her mother's hand and she would not let go; and howl, holy Christ, I swear you could hear her four blocks away. I'd say that it took my father and me a full two minutes to pry those two hands, the living and the dead, apart. Then, later, at the cemetery, I swear again that if it hadn't been for my father's vigilance, and the fact that her spike heels kept getting caught in all that fresh dirt, she would have managed to throw herself into the goddamn hole after the box was lowered. Poor Maureen, it's a terrible thing.

[*Slide of the word* Guilt *appears*]

[*Throughout the next scene the performer assembles the obelisk portion of the monument*]

'The sea, with such a storm ... would have buoyed up and quenched the stellèd fires.' That is from *King Lear*. If I were quoting that line in the Maritimes, I would say it somewhat differently: 'The sea, with such a storm ... would have boo-eed up and quenched the stellèd fires.' 'Boo-ee!' On Prince Edward Island you could cause a real panic if you said, 'Oh my, look at that "boy" floating out there in the harbour.' You just never know the subtle ways in which the pronunciation of a single word might have an effect. For example, last summer, while wandering on the East Coast, I decided to write some haiku—you know—those lovely, simple Japanese poems that must conform to two strict rules: they must have exactly seventeen syllables, and they can't have any abstract thought. Anyway, I was very upset when I realized that the best one that I had written—'I swim in sea-grey water past marker boo-ees and yellow dories'—wouldn't be a haiku anymore when I got it back to Ontario.

But for me, buoy's richness as a word doesn't just come from its pronunciation, it has all kinds of other meanings and associations. Literally, a buoy is an object anchored as an aid to navigation, or to indicate dangers like hidden wrecks or rocky shoals.

[A sequence of slides begins, and continues throughout this section about buoys. That is, until the monument is completed]

Even though a buoy is anchored, it still moves; it sways and bobs and rings its message: 'this way, over here, careful, careful, watch your step.' As a verb, 'buoy' means to raise, or lift, or to cause to rise. There are many kinds of buoys.

[Slides of buoys and of the sea continue]

'Can' buoys, 'nun' buoys, 'spar' buoys, 'gong' and 'bell' buoys. My father worked with buoys for many years—not the kind most of us are familiar with, little wooden or Styrofoam bobbles—he worked with the giant deep-sea buoys that look like missiles and weigh tons. When my siblings and I were kids we thought it was so fabulous that our father had our mother's name on the back of all his overalls—Dot, D.O.T., Department of Transport. Underneath that was the romantic phrase 'Boo-ee Maintenance.'

Because buoys took him away for long periods of time to exotic places like Baffin Island and the Arctic Circle, I think we all developed a relationship to the 'idea' of buoys. For me, they conjured up images of clanging bells, flashing lights, high, stormy waves and great winches turned by sailors' arms. In later years, I always intended to talk to my father about his years on the sea, but like most other conversations I had ever imagined having with him, I never quite got around to it. Oh, I know how that must sound, you're probably thinking, 'Poor baby, couldn't talk to his daddy—how unique.' I honestly don't mean to whine, it's just that not being able to talk to my father about buoys somehow came to represent all of the things that I had never been able to talk to him about—boy oh boy— I mean, talk about investing things with meaning. I did eventually broach the subject with him, and I guess I was expecting beautifully constructed metaphors about his life of the high seas; what I got, of course, was a tired man describing a very difficult job that kept him away from his family in order to support them. A different set of meanings to be sure. But I guess I finally clued in to the fact that, for me at least, buoys are my father, and that part of my childhood that he represents.

[*End of monument assembly for now. End of slide sequence*]

[*The performer once again sits in his tree-chair for the following story*]

When Louie Herman died, Tina called in a big panic and Dad had to go up the road to help her out. We all knew that something was wrong because Dad actually walked and, like most men in the country, he always drove anywhere further away than the end of our own lane. Now—Tina and Louie, along with their retarded daughter Louise, were just about the most comical trio you'd ever want to meet. Tina and Louie liked to stay up all night with a quart of Captain Morgan's and a pack of well-worn cards, and then, at about four or five in the morning, they'd wake up Louise and the three of them would traipse down to the shore, and they'd all go fishing in Louie's yellow dory. So—this particular morning, Louie pulls on those big fishing boots, and dies, right there in the kitchen; which I personally do not think he would have complained about if he had been in a position to do so. The big problem with arranging Louie's funeral was that they couldn't find a box in town big enough to put him in, or, as it turns out, in the whole damn province. Sinclair Cutcliffe, the cheapest, meanest undertaker in town, offered to cut the end out of a coffin and stick a piece on, but we all agreed that would be pretty friggin' tacky, so Dad says, 'It's okay Tina, it's okay. Delmar and I,'— Delmar was Tina's nephew—'Delmar and I will get in the wagon and drive over to Moncton and get a box for Louie,' which they did. Tina always loved to tell this story about how Louie was too damn big for any box in Prince Edward Island, and she told it as if she knew how much Louie would have loved that story, too.

[*Slide of the word* Love *appears*]

[*During the next scene, the set and lights conspire to create an atmosphere of bleak confinement*]

'Our block was occupied only by homosexuals, with about two hundred and fifty men in each wing. We could only sleep in our night-shirts, and we had to keep our hands outside the blankets … The windows had a centimetre of ice on them. Anyone found with his underclothes on in bed, or his hands under his blanket … was taken outside and had several bowls of water poured over him before being left standing outside for a good hour. Only a few people survived this treatment. The least result was bronchitis, and it was rare for any gay person taken into the sick-bay to come out alive. We who wore the pink triangle were prioritised for medical experiments, and these generally ended in death.'

That's a quote from a book called *The Men with the Pink Triangle*, written by a concentration-camp survivor by the name of Heinz Heger. Most of us know, I think, that all prisoners in German concentration camps during the Second World War had triangles of coloured cloth sewn onto their uniforms to denote their offence or their origin, which, in some cases, was their only offence. Yellow was for the Jews, who got two triangles superimposed to make the Star of David. Red was for politicals, green for criminals, black for anti-socials, purple for Jehovah's Witnesses, blue for immigrants, brown for Gypsies, and pink was for homosexuals. This pink triangle was two or three centimetres larger than all of the others, and the prisoners who were the most tortured and persecuted, according to Heinz Heger, were the Jews, the Gypsies and the homosexuals.

The word 'survival' is a word with a great variety of significances. If you were to ask the survivor of a concentration camp about survival, the answer would surely relate to their wartime experiences. 'Survival' has one set of meanings in the natural world, and quite a different significance when considered as a cultural term. Since the end of World War II, we have even created a situation where the term 'global survival' has a very real and particular meaning.

[*The atmosphere 'lifts' a little, and the performer becomes more relaxed, now sitting near the audience*]

It is a difficult thing for most of us to credit that which we perceive as overwhelming with any sense of immediacy; it's

Ken Garnhum in *Beuys Buoys Boys*
Photographer: Michael Cooper

easier to say, 'Why bother?' I have personally always had a pretty romantic notion of survival; as a child my favourite book was *Robinson Crusoe;* I longed to test my own ingenuity, to make an umbrella that worked, practically *and* aesthetically. But lately my understanding of survival has undergone a change. For instance, I have not just been ignoring, but I have actually been embracing the oppression that comes with being a gay man in this society. What I mean is—I feel so damn guilty about being a First World, white, able-bodied *male* person, that my oppression as a 'faggot' is almost welcome to me. It alleviates my guilt by making me a part of the oppressed masses.

There are many kinds of holocausts, some natural and others man-made, but I think, perhaps, that there are really only two possible reactions to any holocaust. Which is more human— 'compassion,'

[*Slide of the word* Compassion *appears*]

or 'complicity?'

[*Slide of the word* Complicity *appears*]

[*Once again, the performer wraps himself in felt*]

'One day you'll be blind, like me. You'll be sitting there, a speck in the void, in the dark, forever, like me.'

[*It gets quite dark*]

'One day you'll say to yourself, I'm tired, I'll sit down, and you'll go and sit down. Then you'll say, I'm hungry, I'll get up, and get something to eat. But you won't get up. You'll say, I shouldn't have sat down, but since I have I'll sit on a little longer, then I'll get up and have something to eat ... You'll look at the wall a while, then you'll say, I'll close my eyes, perhaps have a little sleep ... and you'll close them. And when you open them again there'll be no wall any more. [*pause*] Infinite emptiness will be all around you, all the resurrected dead of all the ages wouldn't fill it, and there you'll be like a little bit of grit in the middle of the steppe.'

[*The performer runs out of felt. Now he creates the room and the Action he is about to describe. He speaks, first referring to the passage he has just quoted*]

Samuel Beckett again—*Endgame*—it makes me think of Joseph Beuys. Beuys was a bomber pilot in the German army during the Second World War. He was wounded five times, and the last time, he was shot down on the Russian Steppes, from which, he says, he was rescued by Tartars and wrapped in fat and felt to help him survive. There is a degree of speculation in the art world regarding the veracity of the story, but real or half-imagined, this particular experience was the catalyst for a body of work that was compulsively concerned with survival. Beuys spoke openly and eloquently about the war and his experiences in it; he did not believe in hiding history. For Joseph Beuys that 'little bit of grit in the middle of the steppe' must speak. He spoke often of 'healing processes' and, for him, the greatest healing process of all was the making of art.

[*Action begins*]

It is November, 1965, and you are in Dusseldorf in West Germany. You have been invited to an opening at the Gallery Schmele, but when you arrive you find yourself barred from entering the gallery. There is only one door into the exhibition space, and one window at street level. There are already a great number of people gathered, and it is difficult to find a place. Finally, you find a little niche from which you can see into the room. Now you see that there is a man in this room, a man whose head is covered in honey and gold leaf. An iron sole is tied to his right foot, a felt sole to his left. In his arms the man is cradling a dead hare. For the next three hours the man will walk around the gallery whispering explanations of his pictures to his lifeless burden.

And you think, 'Is he nuts, or what?' You are slightly offended by your exclusion; you are being kept on the outside. But at the same time you do have to admit that there is something compelling about this man—his gravity, his apparent, almost painful, concern, his dedication to his task. The honey and gold leaf glisten and trickle, and the man's mouth is moving, silent and serious. And suddenly you want to know what this man is telling, and at the same moment you know that you cannot know; it is unknowable. Oh—how we long for explanations.

[*End of Action*]

I will tell you some things I have seen:
A black lacquer vase with willow weeping
One hundred yellow freesia in a clear crystal sphere
A single rose
A burning candle
A candid photograph
Pungent sprays of lilac in the middle of winter.
Faces, whispers, hands hover
The polished granite cubes of ashes
In lofts full of men full of martinis
And a wild, aching desire for living.

Laughing or wailing, public or private, music-filled or silent—a memorial service is a memorial service is a memorial service; and boys will be boys will be dying. The older I get the more I am clinging to the boy in me. It is a wonderfully rich word for one so short—'boy.' It is full of a kind of energy, a lightness, a vulnerability.

It is said that there are stages to the act of dying: resignation, spirituality, anger, I think. I do not know them all, nor do I know their order. I do not know. I do know that there are stages to watching death, and anger is one of those. This is something else that I have seen: I have seen the valiant and necessary attempts to celebrate life in the face of death begin to have a hollow ring.

[*The performer sets about returning the stage to its original state in preparation for the final stage of the assembly of the monument*]

There are people in this world who believe that they hold the patent on love. They know to whom they have sold franchises, and from whom they have withheld them. These love capitalists are real people, too; they are Real Women and real Prime Ministers and real former figure-skaters. But—I know something. I know that 'love' is hiding a pair of great, black wings, and when she unfolds them, and flies up and up into our dark and carking atmosphere, she will be abandoning us all —every one; and while she is still with us, nobody holds the exclusive rights.

[*The performer comes across a final* Barbie's Beckett. *Barbie is dirty and damaged. Her hair is falling out. What little clothing she has is torn*]

Well—what do you know—Barbie does *Endgame*; looks like a real performance art production, too. 'Finished, it's finished, it must be nearly finished. [*pause*] Grain upon grain, one by one, and one day, suddenly, there's a heap, a little heap, the impossible heap.'

[*The performer places Barbie on the seat of the tree-chair. Then he tips the now-empty cart onto its side and removes the wheel unit from its underside. This unit is then fitted under the tree-chair. This new wheeled unit can now be used by the performer to take things away as he exits at the end of the piece]*

One of Joseph Beuys' last major works before he died was a project called *7,000 Eichen* (*Seven Thousand Oaks*), an environmental artwork. As you might surmise from the title, there were indeed seven thousand oak trees, but there were also seven thousand roughly-hewn stone columns, each approximately one metre high. The plan was that these would be planted in pairs, an oak and a basalt column, all around the city of Kassel over a period of time. Beuys planted the first tree in March of 1982. In typical Beuysian fashion, he very grandly declared that *7,000 Eichen* was not only important in terms of 'matter' and 'ecology,' but that it would continue to raise ecological consciousness because, in his words, 'we will never stop planting.' Trees continue to be planted in the name of this project and its architect in cities around the world. Beuys also said that his point in pairing the two elements was that 'each would be a monument, consisting of a living part, the live tree, changing all the time; and a crystalline mass, the basalt column, maintaining its shape size and weight; and that by placing these two objects side by side, the proportionality of the monument would never be the same.' Never be the same.

[The performer stands where the tree-chair had been to deliver this final funeral story]

After arriving like the proverbial ill wind she was, and announcing that Grammy was dead, Aunt Ann said, 'And there's enough money in her purse to pay for the flowers.' Now, Mom and I thought that this was just about the cheapest, most callous thing we had ever heard in our lives, but then, according to Aunt Ann, my mother and I were almost too sensitive to live, anyways. She also told us that Sinclair Cutcliffe had Grammy already. The ceilings of the Cutcliffe Funeral Home are really low, and they are stuccoed, with glitter dust embedded in every plaster stalactite. The wallpaper is that red, flocked stuff, worn black at elbow level by the leaning of tired men. In Grammy's case, however, the worst thing was not the decor of Slumber Room Number One; it was the casket itself. It was kind of flocked too, and blue—blue like nothing natural you've ever seen in your life. I was twelve at the time and I remember thinking, 'Why isn't it wooden, aren't coffins supposed to be made out of wood?' Then I realized that under the layers and layers of powder, my Grandmother was blue too, as blue as the beaverboard box they'd laid her out in.

Crazy Grammy, who wrote to her dead husband every night for nine years; Grammy, who loved oranges and the smell of mothballs, and who hated Catherine MacKinnon more than any other singer in the world. Crazy Grammy, who took every goddamn pill in the house. And I remember thinking, 'Boys oh boys, I would have got her a wooden coffin,' and I wanted to tell everyone who kept coming up and saying how nice she looked to 'shut up, just shut up.'

[*At this point, space—oceanic space, or an illusion of it—is created. The performer places the inverted cart in this space, placing the obelisk on top of it, and the pyramid on top of that. Lights begin to fade as the top of the 'buoy' begins to light up. The performer prepares to exit. By the time he is gone, the buoy is the only light on stage*]

My grandmother always said that 'a full day is a happy day.' So—I guess I was right about this one.

[*Pause. The performer begins to exit*]

Luis Buñuel said that 'life without memory is no life at all; [memory] is our coherence, our reason, our feeling.' In the end, for my grandmother, memory was none of those things. [*pause*] A memory is like a monument, it is a tricky thing; you have to find a place to put it. The site is all-important.

[*Exit*]

[*End*]

Capote at Yaddo

A Very Gay Little Musical

by Sky Gilbert

Capote at Yaddo: A Very Gay Little Musical was first produced by Buddies In Bad Times Theatre and premiered at Factory Theatre Studio Cafe in Toronto in April 1990 with the following cast:

TRUMAN CAPOTE, Peter Lynch
NEWTON ARVIN, Les Porter
MARY ARVIN, Judith Orban
HOWARD DOUGHTY, Robert Dodds

Director, Set and Costume Designer: Sky Gilbert
Composer, Musical Director, and Pianist: John Alcorn
Stage Manager: Steve Clellend
Lighting Designer: Lorne Reid

For permission to perform the play please contact:

Sky Gilbert
552 Church Street
PO Box 105
Toronto, Canada
M4Y 2H0

Characters:

TRUMAN CAPOTE, a twenty-year-old writer
NEWTON ARVIN, an elegant, forty-year-old critic
MARY ARVIN, his charming, intelligent wife
HOWARD DOUGHTY, his intelligent friend

Setting:

Outdoors and indoors at Yaddo, a summer writers' retreat at
Saratoga, New York. The time is 1946.

It's very hard to be a gentleman and a writer.

— SOMERSET MAUGHAM

Capote at Yaddo

Lights up on NEWTON ARVIN. *He sits in a chair, a wine glass dangling forlornly in his hand. He stares off, then speaks*

NEWTON And I see the skaters there
making their fabulous turns
jumping, lost in the air—
laughing, talking, rubbing
their hands in the frosty
cold, and then why, for some
reason—who knows, some memory, some
something from my past—why?
I then ... turn away. And cry.

[*Pause. Blackout. Pause. Lights up on* NEWTON *standing in front of the same chair with the same wine glass rigid in his hand. Beside him is* HOWARD DOUGHTY, *and beside* HOWARD *is* NEWTON*'s wife,* MARY ARVIN. *All stand stiff and erect in formal clothes. They sing, staring out directly at the audience, with no attempt at casual naturalism*]

ALL It started out one summer
when the days were very hot
NEWTON Not cold at all
ALL It's in summertime, you know, that
human memories are made
HOWARD I'm very tall
NEWTON & MARY You're very tall

NEWTON And so am I

NEWTON & MARY [*turning to* HOWARD]
    We love you for
    your brain, your wits
    your slow deliberation
    the painful silence of
    your smile
    your sweet vituperation
    We love you when
    you talk historically
    ourselves into a stupor
    but most of all we love you
    'cause you look like
    Gary Cooper!

HOWARD Don't talk of me

NEWTON & MARY Why not?

HOWARD Talk of

ALL Capote, Capote
    Capote at Yaddo
    He came one summer
   · and destroyed our lives!
    Capote at Yaddo!
    It started out one summer
    when the days were very hot

NEWTON Not cold at all

ALL It's in summertime, you know, when
    painful memories are made

NEWTON He's very short

HOWARD & MARY Who's very short?

NEWTON Capote

ALL We loved him for
    his shortness, for
    his stature so minute

his youth and for his beauty
which perhaps was not astute
But just because the books we
write are about
Hawthorne, Melville and Whitman
so what—we're even more susceptible
to love's pernicious quicksand
HOWARD Don't talk of Capote!
NEWTON & MARY Why not?
ALL We must talk of
    Capote, Capote
    Capote at Yaddo
    He came one summer
    and destroyed our lives!
    Capote at Yaddo!
    Oh, we'll never forget that summer
    when our love was very hot
NEWTON Not cold at all …
ALL And we had such hatred for each other
    that our lives began to rot
HOWARD Why did he do it?
MARY He didn't mean to
NEWTON Yes he did—
ALL Youth is it's own excuse
    It
    means no harm but when
    it
    loves you'd better get
    out of the way or else
    I'm sorry, that's
    it
    you're caught trapped contemplating
    it!

Robert Dodds (HOWARD), Les Porter (NEWTON), and Judith Orban (MARY)
Photographer: David Hawe

writing about
it!
wanting to hold
it!
touch
it!
caress
it!
make
it
understand
which
it
never will because
it's
youth
it's
Capote, Capote
Capote at Yaddo
He came one summer
And destroyed our lives!
Capote at Yaddo!

[*Lights up on a young* TRUMAN CAPOTE. *He is wearing a long shirt and jeans and sneakers, and looks charming. He sits on the edge of the stage with his legs hanging*]

TRUMAN I am incredibly willing to consider the possibility that I am not a genius. The possibility. But I guess the thing is that if I'm not a genius then what's this pain for? And why am I so weird? I suppose I could be just one of nature's freaks which I suppose I am, no matter what and maybe all this artiste junk is just a way of justifying it, you know? Well anyway the point is I've written a couple of short stories and

they are absolutely fabulous and I've got this gift and people
stare at me and I like it. I like being stared at why shouldn't I?
Don't you like the way I talk? Do you think it's weird? Well
I think you're weird so there everybody is weird my friend
Carson McCullers is the weirdest of all. Just think for a
minute what it would be like to be a boy and look like me
and act like me. [*pause*] Just think. [*pause*] Do you know
what my mother used to do to me when I was a kid? She used
to make me wear wrist splints. You know why? So that I
would keep my wrists straight. And I'll never forget one day
when I wanted to wear a red kerchief around my neck and
I went to her and asked her if I could wear it or if it looked
weird because I thought maybe it didn't I didn't know fem-
inine or masculine then. I just thought maybe it was bad to
wear that kerchief I don't know why. And she told me it was.
She wouldn't let me wear it. She always wanted me to be like
the other boys, but I'm not. But you know something? Some
of the other boys like me. And you know what the other boys
want to do? They want to fuck me. And they want it so bad
… and sometimes I give it to them and sometimes I don't.
But I'm not fickle that is I like … I like … what do I like …
I like the smart ones. With big dicks. If they're smart and
they have big dicks then they're perfect. And with women it's
something else because with men I don't know I just want a
big one to put his arms around me but with women it's
different I love them differently they're so graceful and
beautiful and I love them when they're smart and I want to
help them and make them happy but I don't want to have sex
with them. So maybe I cause trouble. So maybe a lot of
people don't like me because they think I'm trying to make
an impression. So maybe I am. So maybe life imitates art. So
maybe life is art. So maybe you've got to live so intensely that
you could just die or else you don't have anything to write

about. So maybe you have to be on stage all the time because that's artifice and that's what you're writing about so you do it and be it and then write about it. But then again I don't have to justify myself to you. I can be arrogant. *I am an artist!* But sometimes I just think I'm ... just a ... a ... brat. But I'm not ... no ... that's just a joke. I'm really very profound. You don't believe me? I can prove it ... don't worry ... I know you don't have to be profound to ruin people's lives but you have to be profound to ruin their lives and then make them love you afterwards. And I can do that. The day I can't do that, I'm dead. Just like that. You turn that screw, make 'em go ouch, but then they've just gotta love ya. That means you're very special. Very weird, and it also means ... you're a genius. See. I told ya I was. I told you.

[*Lights dim on* TRUMAN. *Up on* NEWTON, HOWARD, *and* MARY *lounging in their formal clothes on the summer lawns at Yaddo, drinks in their hands*]

MARY Now let me try and fully understand this point.

NEWTON [*sipping*] Ah yes, do, please do.

MARY It's something to do with a definition of comedy of manners?

HOWARD [*gesturing, negative*] Ughghghgh.

MARY Ughghghgh what?

HOWARD Ughghghgh no.

MARY No what?

HOWARD Not a definition.

NEWTON No, not a definition, really, just where can it be, where can it rest ...

HOWARD That's a line from *Hamlet* ... Claudius intones ... 'what rests' ...

NEWTON Yes ... My query is, where does comedy of manners rest, where can it be, why didn't Shakespeare write the comedy of manners, for instance?

MARY [*almost a question*] He was too profound.

HOWARD [*laughing*] That's funny.

MARY I have an undergraduate sense of humour, Howie.
I almost got kicked out of Smith for it.

NEWTON [*smiling*] It's true. It's quite an honour almost to get
kicked out of Smith.

MARY Yes Howie, it was so funny. I said I didn't like Shaw,
and one of my professors told me that was an undergraduate
response, not to like something was an undergraduate
response. Howie I couldn't—

NEWTON Don't call him Howie.

HOWARD I don't mind.

NEWTON You say you don't but you do.

HOWARD I don't.

MARY Alright, Howard, but back to—

NEWTON Comedy of manners—

MARY Yes … Dotty? Shall I call you Dotty?

HOWARD I don't mind—

NEWTON He minds everything, he just doesn't say it—

HOWARD Maybe I don't, maybe I'm different than you, maybe
everyone isn't the same as you, Newton.

MARY Now there's an idea, everybody isn't an incredibly
tedious, exacting intellectual with a heart of Jello. Is that
possible? Do you think that's possible? Darling? Love me still?

NEWTON [*with friendly disapproval*] We were discussing—

HOWARD & MARY comedy of manners— [*they laugh*]

NEWTON And my point is, you need a rigid social code in order
to have it—

MARY Well, the Elizabethans had a social code—

HOWARD But it was crumbling—all that Renaissance stuff—
you know, the birth of reason wreaking its havoc on
Medieval mysticism—

MARY I never thought of it that way—

HOWARD But what about the Restoration.

NEWTON What about it.

MARY I know what Howie, I mean ... Mr. Doughty, means.

HOWARD Thank you, Mrs. Arvin.

MARY You're terribly welcome— I mean there may have been social codes in the Restoration but there was this underbelly of sleaze—

NEWTON [*getting excited*] But that is my essential point don't you see? Social codes ultimately don't work so there is always an underbelly of sleaze, as you so undergraduately put it, and that's what comedy of manners is about—it's the bestial reality fighting to get out of the social codes, rearing its ugly head—

MARY To choose an all-too-overused metaphor—

HOWARD So wait a minute.

NEWTON Yes.

MARY [*to* NEWTON] That's very smart, darling. I love that theory, it's so neat—

NEWTON I know. What Howard?

HOWARD Wait a minute.

NEWTON Wait a minute, what.

MARY I love the way Howard makes a point.

NEWTON So do I, you just have to stop and listen. Now wait a minute what?

[NEWTON & MARY *stare at* HOWARD]

HOWARD If social codes don't work, then how do you keep society going? How do you run it? What governs moral behaviour? What happens to ethics?

NEWTON Ahh ... you see ... you get to my big theory, my pet theory.

MARY [*staring at him over her glass*] Which is ...

NEWTON Obsession.

HOWARD What?

MARY [*laughs*] What?

NEWTON Obsession. That is the real moral order. That is the true categorical imperative. The raison d'être of every human action, if you will. It's in *Moby Dick* it's in Hawthorne it's why we do things—because we are obsessed.

MARY With what?

NEWTON With whatever we are obsessed with.

MARY What a strange theory for you to come up with.

NEWTON Why.

MARY Then what's your obsession.

NEWTON Truth.

HOWARD Is it?

NEWTON [*sharply*] Yes.

[*Pause. They stare at each other.* TRUMAN *appears at the top of a stairway leading to their patio. He stares at them for a moment*]

MARY [*giggles*] Oh look.

NEWTON What?

MARY [*whispers*] Shhh ... there ... it's a little boy.

HOWARD [*looking*] Where—

MARY There. Watching us. [*she points*]

[*They all stare at him. Pause*]

TRUMAN I'm not a little boy.

MARY What was that?

TRUMAN I said I'm not a little boy. I'm Truman Capote.

NEWTON [*astonished*] Truman ...

TRUMAN That's me. [*he steps up*] And who are you?

NEWTON Why, I'm ... [*he gets up*] I'm Newton Arvin.

MARY [*getting up*] I'm Mary Arvin.

HOWARD [*getting up also*] I'm Howard Doughty.

TRUMAN It's nice to meet you.

[*Pause. They stare at him*]

You can sit down now.

NEWTON I'm sorry.

[*They sit*]

TRUMAN That's alright, you don't have anything to be sorry for—

MARY We were expecting ... I don't know what we were expecting—

NEWTON Someone ... older, I suppose—

TRUMAN I'm twenty years old.

MARY That's very nice.

TRUMAN [*pause*] You shouldn't treat me like a little boy. I'm not one. I'm very smart. I have very important things to say.

MARY We understand.

TRUMAN Do you?

MARY Well, that is, I—

TRUMAN Are you two married?

NEWTON Why, yes—

TRUMAN I thought maybe you were brother and sister.

MARY No ... we're married.

[*Awkward pause*]

TRUMAN Oh. [*turns to* HOWARD] You look like Gary Cooper.

HOWARD [*shyly*] I know.

TRUMAN Are you a writer?

HOWARD We're all writers.

TRUMAN Do you want to go for a walk?

HOWARD Who?

TRUMAN You.

HOWARD Ahhh ... well ...

TRUMAN If you don't, that's okay.

HOWARD [*pause*] Would you two ...

NEWTON & MARY No ... don't mind us ... we're just talking ... feel free [*ad lib more*]

TRUMAN I hope I'm not interrupting. I just want to talk with you about art.

HOWARD Sure.

TRUMAN Good. You guys don't mind?

NEWTON & MARY No ... we don't mind at all ... ignore us ... see you later ...

TRUMAN Bye. It was nice meeting you Mr. and Mrs. Arvin.

NEWTON & MARY Ah yes, lovely meeting you too ... don't mention it ... bye ...

HOWARD Goodbye.

NEWTON Goodbye Howard.

[*They walk off. Pause*]

MARY [*gets up and stares after them. Lets out a strange laugh*] He thought we were brother and sister. Can you believe that? [*pause. She turns to* NEWTON] From the mouths of babes.

NEWTON [*very angry, hurt*] Mary, please—

MARY Please what. [*angrily*] Are you going to tell me not to be vulgar, is that what you're going to do? Don't be vulgar Mary is that what you're going to say? Well no such luck honey I am vulgar, oh yes I'm a fishwife I am. [*pause*] Do you suppose they're going to fuck in the woods?

NEWTON [*aghast*] Mary.

MARY Why not? He's a pretty little thing. If I had a dick I'd fuck him. And imagine ... if he actually has a mind ... or does it matter? Imagine the two of them together ... in the woods ... getting dirty, rustling the leaves ...

NEWTON [*gets up*] Excuse me.

MARY What's the matter darling, do you hate sex that much?

Or are you just jealous? Is that it? Howard gets the literary prize—the little genius and all—because he looks like Gary Cooper and you don't? Is that it?

[*She grabs him*]

Is it?

NEWTON Let go of my arm.

MARY Is it that awful for me to touch you? Is it?

NEWTON [*tortured*] No.

MARY Oh, there.

[*She lets go*]

Newton.

NEWTON [*stops at the door. Not looking at her*] Yes.

MARY If you're going to go to your room and cry—which is what I think you're going to do—the walls in this summer place are paper thin you know—if that's what you're going to do, at least allow me to come and hold your hand, at least? Will you allow me that?

NEWTON [*shading his eyes*] I'm sorry.

[*He runs off. Pause*]

MARY I bet that's what they are doing. I bet they are ... fucking ...

[*Lights dim on her. Up on* TRUMAN *and* HOWARD *walking through the forest*]

TRUMAN You're taller than me.

HOWARD Yes.

TRUMAN But then I'm not tall.

HOWARD No, you're not.

TRUMAN I like that.

HOWARD Good.

TRUMAN [*pause*] So you're a writer.

HOWARD Yes. We all are.

TRUMAN What are you writing.

HOWARD A biography of Frances Parkman.

TRUMAN Who's she?

HOWARD *He's* an historian.

TRUMAN That sounds interesting.

HOWARD Does it?

TRUMAN No. But then I'm not very cultured. I'm just intelligent. I'm writing a novel. It's my first.

HOWARD How's it going?

TRUMAN Fine. I'm about halfway through. It's about my childhood sort of. And all the weird people I knew. Do you know Carson?

HOWARD McCullers?

TRUMAN Yeah. She's just about the only person in the world as weird as me. She got me an agent. They gave me an advance. Now I have to write the book.

HOWARD I think you will.

TRUMAN Do you?

HOWARD Yes.

TRUMAN [*pause*] Could you ... hold me.

HOWARD Yes.

[*Pause.* HOWARD *holds* TRUMAN]

TRUMAN There ... that feels good. I like it when guys bigger than me hold me. [*pause*] Do you kiss like Gary Cooper?

HOWARD I don't know. I've never kissed him.

TRUMAN But you like to kiss guys, don't you.

HOWARD Yes. How did you know?

TRUMAN You can tell.

HOWARD How.

TRUMAN By the way you look at me.

HOWARD With desire.

TRUMAN Yeah, I guess. [*pause*] So go ahead. Kiss me.

[*They kiss. It is passionate*]

How was that?

HOWARD Very nice.

TRUMAN Do it again.

[*They kiss again. Pause*]

Can I tell you something?

HOWARD Sure.

TRUMAN If we have sex, it would be just like that, that's all, just having sex. I mean you're very sexy. But that's all it would be because ... well I think that's it. That's all.

HOWARD I understand.

TRUMAN Is that alright?

HOWARD Sure.

TRUMAN Then let's go.

[*They kiss. The lights dim. Up on* NEWTON *in his room, alone, staring out the window. He sings*]

NEWTON And it was winter
I was alone in my room
my usual room
my usual stare
no one there
and
out my window
in the winter
there were skaters
on the pond
the ineffable
indescribable
indestructible

laughter
of fun being had
of memories being made
but me

So here I am
watching
what does it take
to be
always standing by
watching
when will I, if ever
just be
He's a boy with a will and a want and a wish of his own
He's a boy with a genius a talent that's easy to see
He's a boy fucking Howard as I sit at my window and muddle
He's a boy who I'll love and who'll never even look at me

And it's winter
for me all the time
my usual pain
my usual sadness
how do I stand it
and outside my window
in the woods
boys are making love
under the trees
the ineffable
indescribable
indestructible
taste
of love being made
of memories being made
but me

Why am I always
watching
this time at last
I'll be
no one is meant for
watching
everyone is meant
to be
He's an uncanny boy there'll not be another like him
He's as funny and as sunny and as real and as sweet as a peach
He's a boy who's someone else's as long as I sit here and dawdle
He's a boy a brilliant boy dammit, he's in my reach!

It could be summer
I might not be alone
that unusual love
that unusual lust
could it be mine?

[*A knock at the door*]

    [*speaks*] Come in!

HOWARD [*ebullient, which is not his usual state*] It's me.

NEWTON Oh. Howard.

HOWARD Did I hear you just say something?

NEWTON Well—

HOWARD Did you say ... it could be summer?

NEWTON Well, I don't know. I was all alone ... one of my
moods. I could have been muttering to myself—

HOWARD [*sitting down beside him*] No Newton no. It *is* summer,
I guarantee it, it is most definitely summer.

NEWTON Why Howard?

HOWARD What.

NEWTON You seem almost ... enthusiastic. [*looking at him*

nastily] It's most uncharacteristic of you. I don't think I like it.

HOWARD Oh Newton Newton Newton. [*almost jumping up and down*]

NEWTON What is it boy— Sit—

HOWARD I can't he's just so ... he's just so ... beautiful ... do you have any idea how beautiful he is?

NEWTON We wouldn't by chance, be talking about Truman Capote would we?

HOWARD Oh yes yes yes ... he's just ... he's an angel an absolute angel, so tender, so loving, so passive, yet aggressive ... grrrrrrr [*he growls*] I've never quite had sex with anyone like that.

NEWTON Well well well. [*pause*] He fucked you did he?

HOWARD No ... can you believe it? I fucked him. I can almost never do that—

NEWTON How very true.

HOWARD But for some reason I just ... got it up, and boy did I get it up and boy I mean ... well boy ... we found this clearing and the light was absolutely—you know I remember reading somewhere about when young, unmarried women go to Rome they often faint when they're looking at Michelangelo's David or a Carvaggio or any of the great nudes, they just become overcome with unrequited lust I guess—and when we were making love in the glade and I was on top of him it was as if ... for a moment I was one of those unmarried ladies and he was ... I don't know the Sistine Chapel, and I almost fainted from the absolute wonder of it all, of him of—

NEWTON [*with anger building*] I don't think you've got that quite right.

HOWARD What?

NEWTON Well if you're on top of him, wouldn't that make you the Sistine Chapel? I could see you being on top of him if he was Napoleon's Tomb, it just seems you've got your metaphors rather mixed—

116

HOWARD I don't care I don't care I don't care. Literary criticism I don't care. I don't care if I don't write another word. I just don't care.

NEWTON [*tight-lipped*] Obviously.

HOWARD Oh Newton Newton Newton I'm so happy I could spit!

NEWTON Well, just don't spit, please, save that for Truman.

HOWARD Newton.

NEWTON Yes.

HOWARD What's wrong.

NEWTON Nothing's wrong.

HOWARD Oh yes there is. Oh no. Are you upset?

NEWTON Me, upset? I'm suicidal. But I'm not upset.

HOWARD Oh my God, what's wrong. Oh no, don't tell me, you're jealous.

NEWTON Me, jealous?

HOWARD Yes, but I don't understand, I thought we worked it out. I thought we both said that we had reached the stage in our relationship where we could both fool around.

NEWTON Well, we certainly seem to have reached it, haven't we?

HOWARD But we said—

NEWTON I know what we said.

HOWARD Oh I see, it's different when it's right under your nose and at Yaddo and everything and we'll all have dinner and everything and discuss art all the time and how embarrassing and why didn't I think. I'm sorry Newton.

NEWTON It's not that.

HOWARD It's not?

NEWTON No.

HOWARD Oh, then what is it then, are you mad that I fucked him? That I fucked him and I never fuck you? But you don't like to get fucked.

NEWTON Don't be vulgar.

HOWARD Well if it's not that then what is it then.

NEWTON I don't want to talk about it.

HOWARD Oh Newton come on, you can't just stay mad—

NEWTON I stay mad all the time, no one seems to have any idea how mad I constantly am. I suppose two suicide attempts don't give you the slightest idea of how incredibly uncontrollably angry I am all the time? Really sometimes it's so unbearable I could just [*he turns away, overcome. Pause*]

HOWARD [*stares at him*] I'm sorry. I mean ... I don't know what to say. I'm sorry.

NEWTON [*still looking away*] It's alright.

HOWARD No, it's not. Really, I don't want you to be so upset, if you'd just tell me.

NEWTON Alright I'll tell you. You want to hear it I'll tell you. And it's totally ridiculous and totally ludicrous but maybe if I don't leave it all bottled up inside of me, then, maybe then, it won't lead to me swallowing a bottle of Nembutals this time. So I'm going to say it and you can laugh or say anything you want to about it—perhaps I'm a ridiculous figure, I'm certain Mary would say I was, if she knew—yes I am totally ludicrous so laugh if you want to. It's inappropriate and impossible but ... I'm in love with him. There, I said it.

HOWARD [*pause*] With who.

NEWTON With— Truman.

HOWARD You are?

NEWTON Yes.

HOWARD But you just met him.

NEWTON So— You just met him and you just fucked him!

HOWARD I know, but that's different.

NEWTON How is it different?

HOWARD Well because ... well lust happens quickly, love takes time to develop. You're sure it's not lust?

NEWTON Oh Howard.

HOWARD What.

NEWTON What a perfectly stupid thing to say—

HOWARD People mistake love and lust all the time—

NEWTON I'll tell you the difference between love and lust. There's the lawn boy. Alright? You know the lawn boy? That Latin fellow with the big bottom and the curly hair. Who struts around as if he owned the place instead of just working here? Yes I would like to do all the nasty things with him and I would feel horribly afterwards and it probably would be horrible and he'd probably have the same contempt for me as he would have for his … woman, and I simply want to see his member, that's all. I would pay for that, and probably some day, I will, but with Truman I have only seen him once, and it's as if there is a halo around his head, and that halo is a mixture of innate intelligence, and sensitivity and pain, can you not feel his pain, in his brave little smile, in that boyish bravado, the absolute craving to be loved, he wants so desperately to be loved even though on the outside he's screaming, 'I don't care if you love me I don't care at all and I'll be objectionable and even inarticulate in an attempt to' … Have you read his short stories have you read 'Miriam'?

HOWARD No—

NEWTON 'Miriam' is as close to a masterpiece as an American short-story writer is going to get, ever, it's evanescent, it sings, it's light and airy and absolutely dark, it's like Melville only it's not a whale, it's a nightingale—am I making things any clearer? That most certainly must be love? What else can it be but love? He is brilliant he can be a genius, all he needs is a teacher. I am that teacher. I don't want to teach the lawn boy. I just want to sneak a peak at whatever he's got. Now Howard, do you understand the difference?

HOWARD Yes.

NEWTON Good. Because I don't think I could possibly explain it again.

HOWARD So.

NEWTON So, there I've said it. Now I don't know what to do
about it. Nothing, as usual.

HOWARD [*pause*] Will you excuse me for a moment while I go in
a corner and think?

NEWTON Of course.

HOWARD I'll be right back.

[*He goes to a corner in spotlight and sings*]

How much did he really mean to me
that charming boy?
Or is he just the ultimate fuck in the woods
a kind of wind-up toy?
I must be rational
and separate the
dark, done deed
from the cold, clear light of day—
well, if the truth be known
if all is said
(it certainly was done)
I might as well give him away
There was the dark and the leaves and the hush and the woods
and the dirt it was rough it was sweet and it smelled and I
pushed and he shoved and we kind of made love
but it was more like sex!
And will you lose respect
for me
if I admit the truth
it was his youth
and my impetuous organ!
I don't care what you think
As if your shit doesn't stink
I'm donating him

to my favourite charity!
I'm giving him
to Newton

[*He walks out of the spotlight and back to* NEWTON]

[*speaks*] Wait a minute.

NEWTON Yes.

HOWARD Wait Newton, listen.

NEWTON What is it.

HOWARD You want him very much, don't you?

NEWTON I'm in love with him.

HOWARD Yeah. I guess you are. [*pause*] So listen.

NEWTON What is it?

HOWARD Look Newton, I love you. You talk about the difference
between the lawn boy and Truman for you—well you know
how I feel about you, and when it comes to that, well,
Truman's just an ultimate sexual fantasy for me, he's sort of
my lawn boy, and you know how it is with lawn boys when
you have them you don't want them anymore so now I've had
him and [*pause*] I don't want him. And [*pause*] and [*pause*] you
can have him.

NEWTON What did you say?

HOWARD I said, you can have him, if you want him. I mean …
now that I've gotten over the initial … thrill— I mean he's
very sweet but if he really means that much to you Newton,
I mean Newton it's you I love, you know that, I would do
anything to stop you from swallowing a bunch of Nembutals,
please, look who cares, he's yours.

NEWTON Are you serious?

HOWARD Of course I'm serious.

NEWTON But how can you just—

HOWARD It's no big deal, really—

NEWTON I'm flabbergasted.

HOWARD I love you Newton. I'd give you anything you wanted. Anything. Take him, take Truman.

[*There is a knock at the door*]

NEWTON Yes?

TRUMAN [*from outside*] It's me, Truman.

NEWTON Oh my God, it's him.

HOWARD Pretty good timing, eh?

NEWTON Wait—

TRUMAN Is there someone there?

NEWTON [*shouting*] Just a minute! [*to* HOWARD] Howard, what do we do?

HOWARD Hey, look, I'll go.

NEWTON Where?

HOWARD I'll climb out the window. It's only one story down.

NEWTON But ... maybe he came to see you—

HOWARD This is your room Newton, for God's sake. He came to see you.

NEWTON But so soon after—

HOWARD But he doesn't know about us, he doesn't know what happened. Maybe he's insatiable.

NEWTON Do you suppose that's possible?

HOWARD Anything's possible.

TRUMAN [*from outside*] Mr. Arvin?

HOWARD He's calling you. Hey, listen ... I love you,

[*He holds* NEWTON]

and anything that happens is okay. Okay?

[*They kiss*]

It's your turn, buddy.

[*He stands at the window*]

Good luck.

[*He climbs out. Pause.* NEWTON *watches him. Another knock*]

NEWTON Coming.

[*He opens the door*]

TRUMAN Hi.

NEWTON Hello.

TRUMAN Did I come at a bad time?

NEWTON No.

TRUMAN I thought I heard voices.

NEWTON Oh, that was me ... Sometimes I ... talk to Herman Melville.

TRUMAN You do?

NEWTON Yes. I'm writing a book about him.

TRUMAN I know. That's neat because sometimes I talk to my characters too. I talk to Joel.

NEWTON Joel?

TRUMAN Joel is the boy in my novel. He loses everything and he grows up. Kind of like Peter Pan.

NEWTON Can I ask you something?

TRUMAN Sure.

NEWTON Why do you affect that childlike way of talking.

TRUMAN It's how I talk.

NEWTON But your writing, I've read it, it's so different—

TRUMAN You read it? You read my story.

NEWTON I read 'Miriam,' yes.

TRUMAN You did?

NEWTON Yes.

TRUMAN Oh my God. I'm so frightened. I want to ask you what you think but I'm too scared.

NEWTON You needn't be.

TRUMAN No.

NEWTON There is the very sure hand of the writer there.

TRUMAN You think so?

NEWTON Yes.

TRUMAN Really?

NEWTON But the darkness ... where does it come from? Where do you find it? You seem so sunny and ... ripe.

TRUMAN I dunno. It's there though. You should meet my family. You should meet my mother. You should meet my Aunt Sook. And my father-who's-never-there-who-wanders. I can be very dark sometimes. But I don't think that's what people want to see so I don't show them that, except in my writing.

NEWTON I respect that darkness.

TRUMAN [*pause*] How long have you known Howard?

NEWTON I've known him for a very long time.

TRUMAN Is he your best friend?

NEWTON Yes.

TRUMAN Your very best friend in the whole world?

NEWTON Yes.

TRUMAN Do you know he's a homosexual?

NEWTON Oh yes.

TRUMAN Does that shock you?

NEWTON No. Perhaps that's why we're friends.

TRUMAN Why does your wife seem so much like your sister?

NEWTON Because we are ... brother and sister in a way. Sometimes marriages become like that, after many years, and that's alright.

TRUMAN Is she in love with you?

NEWTON I think so, very much so.

TRUMAN Are you in love with her?

NEWTON I love her. Perhaps that's a little different.

TRUMAN You know what?

NEWTON What?

TRUMAN I'm all quivering inside.

NEWTON Yes?

TRUMAN Yes. I'm scared of something. I wonder if it's you.
If you could hold me ... then I wouldn't be so scared.

NEWTON Alright, if you wish.

[*He walks over to him and awkwardly puts his arms around him*]

There, is that better?

TRUMAN Yes. Newton?

NEWTON Yes.

TRUMAN Could you teach me some things ... like why Herman
Melville isn't boring?

NEWTON Yes, I could teach you that.

TRUMAN And then ... the dark part of me ... it's not that I want
to tame it it's just ... I want to shape it into something I want to ...

NEWTON It's called style ...

TRUMAN That's it ... I want the style to somehow reflect what
I'm doing more ... I like it when you hold me ...

NEWTON Good ...

TRUMAN Do you like holding me?

NEWTON Yes.

[NEWTON *kisses* TRUMAN. *They look at each other*]

TRUMAN What do we do now?

[*They stare at each other. Pause. The lights dim to black. Lights
up on* TRUMAN *sitting at the edge of the stage. He is looking
mischievous*]

So say it! Say it. Say what you're thinking I know what
you're thinking I do. You think I shouldn't have. You're
making up these rules and saying, 'He's awful.' 'She's awful.'
You are ... stop it don't say those things don't think them you
think it's all a lie and all my feelings for them for both of them
are all just fake lies and not real. They're not. So I slept with

Peter Lynch (**TRUMAN**)
Photographer: David Hawe

both of them in the same day. So *what*. So I did that. So what
does that mean that I'm some sort of horrible person? Grow
up, *girl!* Grow up. I'm not a horrible person I'm just following
my instincts and it all worked out for the best. It did. Howard
and I were—hold back your disapproval—we were just ...
having sex in the woods. That's all. And with Newton and I it
was something else so I know your other accusation—you
think I'm much older and more intelligent than I act and if in
fact I am [*he changes manner*] if in fact I am perfectly aware
[*much more like the older* TRUMAN *we know*] perfectly aware of
exactly the perfidious manipulations which I am exacting on
these poor folk—well that's not completely true. That is, I am
slightly more articulate than I make myself appear but would
Newton fall in love with me if I acted in such a manner? If
I was, in fact, a little Newton—preformed, as it were—would
he take it upon himself to remake me in his image? No ...
Newton is and always will be a teacher, not a writer, though he
wishes to be a writer, yes he is a critic, but that's something
altogether different. But certainly, how could I have appealed
to his passion for patriarchal what shall we say sexual attraction
unless I pretended to be a little bit more malformed than I am.
But let's face it, it's just the lie that tells the truth because I am
malformed, deformed and I do in fact love him and will until
... later ... that is. Dear Newton. But I needed him needed
him to teach me and love me so I acted the part and was the
child because the boy he never had was what he wanted and
that was what I could be so perfectly, physically anyway, and
why fight that? So ... don't look at me with such disapproval.
When I think of myself I think of the third movement of
Tchaikovsky's Sixth Symphony the triumphal march which
was dedicated to youth, but we know it was to a youth, a
particular youth, the spirit of which I embody, and please note
that I couldn't tell you about Tchaikovsky unless Newton

taught me about him which is a case in part for what I'm doing. But now. Now comes my darker part, the part that Newton claims to love but does he love it really? True, he will claim he does because I'm some sort of symbol of some sort of fun that he didn't have on a skating rink in winter but dare I? Dare I speak the truth to Mary? Mary poor lost soul because you will think that I hate her but in fact it is the contrary I love her so much that I feel deep in my darkest soul—and it is very dark, as you will see—that she can must will know the truth and after I tell her I will make her love me for it and why not? Why shouldn't she? Why shouldn't she love the boy that stole the love of her life away? But she never really had him did she? But isn't it better for both of us if she knows the truth? If it isn't then my life ... everything has been ... for nothing ... nothing at all. Which it may be. But who is to say? Not me ... dear child ... dear child that I am not, no, not me.

[*The lights dim on him, come up on* MARY. *She is all alone in a garden somewhere at Yaddo. She gazes out at the scenery.* TRUMAN *enters*]

TRUMAN Hi.

MARY Oh hello.

TRUMAN You're Mary Arvin.

MARY Yes, I am.

TRUMAN We met the first day I was here.

MARY Why, yes, we did.

TRUMAN [*pause*] How are you?

MARY I'm fine.

TRUMAN Good. [*pause*] Have you seen Newton?

MARY I haven't, actually.

TRUMAN Neither have I. I wonder where he is.

MARY Probably in his room, getting depressed.

TRUMAN He does that a lot, doesn't he?

MARY Yes. That's why we love him.

TRUMAN I see. I wasn't sure.

MARY Pardon me?

TRUMAN I wasn't sure why we love him.

MARY [*smiling*] It's just an expression.

TRUMAN I never understand that.

MARY What?

TRUMAN Just an expression, I never know what it means. Words are so important to me I can't imagine why someone would say just an expression, nothing against you but an expression is so important it means so much it expresses what's inside however small it is.

MARY True. [*pause*] But in this case it was just an expression. That is, specifically, if you must know, we don't always love Newton because he's depressed. But the fact of the matter is, he often is. And so it almost becomes endearing, after a while.

TRUMAN Don't you think that's awful?

MARY What?

TRUMAN That he's so sad all the time?

MARY No. I mean, that is … it's Newton. You accept it. One isn't about to change Newton Arvin.

TRUMAN No?

MARY No.

TRUMAN Are you sure?

MARY Quite sure, yes.

TRUMAN You love him very much, don't you?

MARY Yes, I do.

TRUMAN Then why do you stay with him?

MARY [*pause*] What an awful question.

TRUMAN Why?

MARY It is. Don't act innocent with me.

TRUMAN What?

MARY I said don't act innocent with me. Can I be frank?

TRUMAN Please do.

MARY That lost little boy act doesn't go very far with me. I gave up little boys when I was a little girl. I'm interested in men. Men with ideas, with things to say. Not cute little boys.

TRUMAN Alright then. [*pause. He turns and looks at her*] What possible reason could you have for remaining married to your husband, who is a homosexual, and on top of that tortured with conscience. Is that not undeniably selfish? Is it not only for yourself that you remain tied to him? Certainly you prey on his guilt—

MARY Why, you little viper.

TRUMAN I'm not a—

MARY You little cunt. That's what you are isn't it? A little receptacle, a little bumboy. Using Newton, draining all the life out of him. You couldn't give a flying fuck about Newton. All you care about is your fucking career. You couldn't care less whether Newton was in love with you. All you care about is what you can get out of him, no matter how much pain it causes him.

TRUMAN I don't cause him pain—

MARY You will. You know very well you will. When he discovers he's not as young as you. That there are others. That you don't love him as he loves you—

TRUMAN I don't know why you're acting this way. I just want to tell you the truth—

MARY Don't you think I know the truth? Don't you think I knew the truth when I married him? A woman knows by the way a man holds her where his real interests lie. Well, maybe my interests aren't in that area, maybe I'm not a particularly sexual person, maybe I'm quite happy to be his companion not his wife and who are you to say?

TRUMAN Then why do you torture him?

MARY I don't—

TRUMAN Why do you hurt him get angry at him because he pulls away from you because he won't show you everything, because he can't, because he's a homosexual like me.

MARY [*pause*] You little ... shit. [*pause*] Perhaps because ... perhaps because ... I really do truly ... love him. And I don't ... wish to get anything back ... anything at all—

TRUMAN But you do, or else you wouldn't torture him like that—

MARY [*shouting*] *Get away from me! You little snake!* You who holds the truth—has anyone ever told you you're an odious, manipulative adult masquerading as a charming child? Has anyone ever told you that?

TRUMAN Not yet. But they will. I'm sure. They will.

MARY [*pause*] Leave me alone.

TRUMAN [*pause*] Maybe what we have in common is that we both love him.

MARY Maybe what we have in common is that we both need him.

TRUMAN Maybe what we have in common is that we both don't know him.

MARY Maybe what we have in common is that neither of us will ever really have him.

TRUMAN [*pause*] Who does he belong to?

MARY Herman Melville?

[*They both laugh. Pause*]

If you weren't ... my torturer, I might ... actually like you.

TRUMAN Oh, like me. Why not?

MARY I'd rather not.

TRUMAN Why?

MARY It's so perverse.

TRUMAN Be perverse. [*he winks*] Why not?

MARY No, I couldn't. I'm doomed to hate you.

TRUMAN And I'm doomed to pester you from afar.

MARY Well, then we know our place. It's an ordered world.

TRUMAN God help it if we were to be friends.

MARY We won't be.

TRUMAN Are you sure?

MARY Go away. [*she puts her hand up to her mouth*]

TRUMAN What is it?

MARY You make me laugh, I suppose.

TRUMAN [*pleased with himself*] I do?

MARY It's just because you're so precocious. Trapped in this child's body. I'll get over it.

TRUMAN Friends?

MARY Oh, let's not be friends. Let's be on speaking terms.

TRUMAN Alright. That means now and then we'll speak.

MARY Yes.

TRUMAN I like that.

MARY Good. [*pause*] Now will you leave me alone?

TRUMAN Yes.

[*Pause. He walks out*]

MARY [*sings*]
So that
charming, little viper is concerned that I like him
There's no reason, really, to tell him that's a lie
There's something about him that's rather entertaining
An air of cheerful doom, who knows why?
Oh
it's not easy loving a Newton Arvin
Especially when he doesn't love you back
But it's harder still when your competition
is a cunning, twenty-year-old artistic hack!

I'm in love with a man
who doesn't love me

I'm the sand in his eye
the fly in his tea
In the flick of a hand
he'd say goodbye
I should leave him alone
I don't know why
I'm in love with a man
It's all a lie
I imagine it's grand
I must, or I'll cry
What's worst of all
I've just been had
He's as gay as the day
And I don't mean glad!

So I've
pretended to everyone that I've always known it
That Newton's little quirk is no news to me
But now and then I get so terribly angry
And squelch it all—to retain my dignity
If only my lonely soul was less romantic
As boring as dear Howard Doughty's wife
I could chat, and argue, and be pedantic
And give up sex—like any good little wife!

But
I'm in love with a man
who loves me not
If I break my leg
I should be shot
I'm the prick of a pin
a glance not returned
a dreaded cold
the coffee that's burned

[*faster*] the grass that's too long
a dandelion patch
a freezing north wind
an egg that won't hatch
a train that is late
a dog that is spayed
a fungal infection
an operation delayed
the moon on the wane
rice overcooked
lower-back pain
a captain that's hooked!

I'm in love with a man
who *don't* love me
My grammar is bad
Why shouldn't it be?
[*slower*] I'm in love ... with a man
You've heard it before
I'll stop right now
I'm becoming a bore!
[*slowly*] I'm in love
and he doesn't
love me!

[*Lights dim on* MARY. *Up on* NEWTON *sitting in his lawn chair, with a drink dangling. He is talking to Herman Melville*]

NEWTON Well Herman, what do you think? You can speak honestly. We're alone here. Do you think there is a truth? An answer? A possibility of order? Or is it all existential and all one can really do is be oneself? But what if that self is horrid? What if?

[HOWARD *enters. He is wrapped in a blanket and has Kleenex sticking out of his nose*]

HOWARD Newton?

NEWTON [*startled*] What? Oh.

HOWARD Sorry—

NEWTON You startled me—

HOWARD I know, I'm sorry.

NEWTON I was just talking to Herman Melville.

HOWARD Does he answer? [*sniffle*]

NEWTON No but I think that in his silence ... there is truth.
[*pause*] Why are you dressed like that?

HOWARD I'm sick.

NEWTON Oh, no.

HOWARD Yes. I've got this awful [*sniffle*] cold. I thought it was
hay fever, but I think it's just a cold. And it won't go away,
no matter what I do.

NEWTON Oh, that's horrible.

HOWARD Yes, so ... So, I think I'm going home, or to the Cape,
rather.

NEWTON The Cape.

HOWARD Yes.

NEWTON Provincetown?

HOWARD No, not Provincetown, somewhere quiet, so I can
recuperate.

NEWTON Oh, well, isn't Yaddo quiet enough for you?

HOWARD Well, it would be, but you know ... well, lately it's
been rather, everyone's been drinking and yelling a bit more
than usual—

NEWTON Truman's gatherings—

HOWARD Well, it's not Truman's fault— I mean people just
gather 'round him, it's just he's so appealing to everyone,
I understand, he just gets everyone into a party mood, but I'm
not [*sniffle*] in a party mood.

NEWTON What about your book.

HOWARD Well, I can write it at the Cape as well as here.

NEWTON I suppose you can. [*pause*] Well darling, I'm going to miss you.

HOWARD Will you?

NEWTON Yes, of course, do you doubt it?

HOWARD No, of course not. I didn't mean to—

NEWTON I shall be very lonely without you.

HOWARD Well, you can be with Truman—

NEWTON Yes, but I can't be with Truman *all* the time.

HOWARD No? Though I guess you would if you could.

NEWTON I don't know, Howard. One can get all 'Truman-ed' out, you know.

HOWARD Really. I didn't think that was possible, for you.

NEWTON Of course it is.

HOWARD [*pause*] Well, I'd better get going. I'm really feeling miserable.

NEWTON Oh, I'm so sorry.

HOWARD Don't worry about me.

[*He sniffles and shuffles off*]

NEWTON Howard—

HOWARD Yes?

NEWTON Are you alright, I mean ... about Truman and I?

HOWARD Yes, of course.

NEWTON I mean really? You're not ... upset or anything that it's worked out between us?

HOWARD No Newton. I'm just sick.

NEWTON That's all?

HOWARD Yes. Very sick. [*sniffle*] Bye Newton.

NEWTON Bye Howard.

HOWARD Very sick.

[*He wanders off*]

Very, very sick. Ughghgh.

[*Pause.* NEWTON *is alone*]

NEWTON Herman ... he couldn't be angry, could he? Underneath all those sniffles, he wouldn't be angry would he? [*pause*] Herman? Answer me, Herman?

[MARY *bustles in with her suitcases, all dressed for travel*]

MARY Well darling, how are you doing, having a little chat with Herman Melville are you? Why not Hawthorne or Whitman, I should think Whitman would be more your style these days.

NEWTON Mary.

MARY Yes?

NEWTON You're wearing your travelling suit.

MARY Very observant of you darling, it's because I'm travelling, in fact, I'm leaving you.

NEWTON You're what?

MARY I'm leaving you at last. That's it. Kaput. Kaputski. No more. It's over.

NEWTON Our marriage?

MARY No darling, our marriage was over long ago, but not officially. So I suppose it's best to make it official—I mean our relationship—these mutual self-torture sessions we're engaging in and calling devotion—I've decided to end them once and for all. What's the point.

NEWTON But darling—

MARY Please don't 'darling' me ever again. Only men who fuck me get to call me darling. It's a new rule I have— I just made it up.

NEWTON But I don't understand—

MARY Well first of all, you're a homosexual—

NEWTON Shhh, darling. Do you want someone to hear?

MARY Newton, please, all of Yaddo knows. Do you think they're stupid? All that sneaking off to Truman's cabin does not go unnoticed. And those hickeys on your neck.

NEWTON Oh no, I had no idea.

MARY You and Truman are old gossip Newton, but to be fair,
I've decided I'm not leaving you just because you're a homosexual— I mean, that's certainly a decisive factor, but you
might be an entertaining homosexual, or a bisexual slash
homosexual, if only you weren't so unflinchingly devoted to
this perennial sadness this rather predictable tragedy this *Death
in Venice*-style obsessiveness which is so boring and unbecom-
ing. You're addicted to sadness and a suicidal nostalgia for a
youth you never had in the first place, and which you can thus,
therefore, never recapture. I love you Newton, I will always
love you, and since it's hopeless I must get away.

NEWTON But—

MARY No 'buts' darling—

NEWTON Mary—

MARY Yes—

NEWTON Can I just ask you something?

MARY [*looking at her watch*] I think we have time for one question—

NEWTON Is this because of Truman?

MARY Why, what do you mean?

NEWTON Are you harbouring some sort of anger against Truman?

MARY Truman? [*gives him a fake smile*] But darling. I love
Truman. He's such a charming, precocious child. And what
about that *dark* side of his, isn't that a *treat?* Isn't he fascinating, so young, yet so *dark,* how enthralling?

NEWTON But I thought maybe—

MARY Everybody loves Truman. How could I possibly not love
Truman? Why, I'd say his personality lies somewhere between
Milton Berle and the Spanish Inquisition! Sometimes I think
he's both at once! Bye darling!

NEWTON But—

MARY Goodbye. I've determined to be cheerful and not to cry.
Say goodbye to Howard and the boy wonder, will you? I'll see

you at your book launching when and if you ever finish off the Melville. Have a nice life.

[*She exits. Pause*]

NEWTON Mary, Mary! [*he gives up. Slumps in his chair*] Oh my God. My world is crumbling around me. Herman … what do I do? Is my obsession enough to pull me through?

[*Pause.* TRUMAN *enters, skipping and humming*]

TRUMAN La la la la la la la la la la. [*he stops*] Oh, Newton. What's up?

NEWTON Everyone's leaving me— Howard, Mary. I can't believe it my life is crumbling—

TRUMAN Oh no. I'll miss them, especially Mary. She was always really nice to me, considering. Hey, listen, I've got to rush, I'm having dinner with Katherine Anne Porter—you know how she hated me for so long well now I think she likes me. I think she actually *likes* me.

NEWTON [*bitterly*] Everyone loves you, Truman.

TRUMAN I know, isn't it wonderful, I tell them the truth and they love it. I must be a genius.

NEWTON And what's the truth about me, then?

TRUMAN The truth is … you'll always be unhappy unless you have me to love.

NEWTON Why?

TRUMAN I don't know, something you're missing, a part of yourself, half of yourself, your young self— See you later, I've got to go see Katherine—

NEWTON But Truman, my life is falling apart and you want to … visit a friend—

TRUMAN But this is so important to me, Newton darling. You will forgive me. I'll be back later … I'll be your water sprite in the dead of night— Bye—

NEWTON But Truman— I need you now! Truman! Don't leave
me now— Truman!

[HOWARD *and* MARY *enter. She is carrying her suitcase and*
HOWARD *is still wrapped in his sick-blanket. They step forward
and stand in the same stylized manner as in the beginning, but
now they are a much more motley crew.* NEWTON *remains
slumped in his chair*]

HOWARD & MARY It started out one summer
  when the days were very hot
NEWTON Not cold at all
HOWARD & MARY And we had such hatred for each other
  that our love began to rot
TRUMAN [*enters*] I'm very short
NEWTON & MARY & HOWARD   And so you are
  And so we say
  we love you for your
  cheerful smile
  your lack of human feeling
  the graceful way you jab the knife
  is ever so appealing
  We love you for when
  you demand of us
  our love uncompromising
  and tell us all these
  hateful truths that
  tend to leave us lying
  in the gutter, and of loving quite without
  our rightful portion
  Boiling in oil's too good for you—
  you scheming little abortion!
TRUMAN Don't talk of me
NEWTON & MARY & HOWARD   Why not?

TRUMAN Talk of—

NEWTON & MARY & HOWARD Capote, Capote
  Capote at Yaddo
  He came one summer
  and destroyed our lives!
  Capote at Yaddo!

TRUMAN [*speaks over the music*]
  The point is that
  you love me
  though your hearts
  are filled with hate
  and though I'm loathe to leave you
  in this unpleasant state
  the truth is I must make my exit
  and though that's a bitter pill
  I'll sugar-coat it and
  I'll make you smile
  and you will love me still
  Bye!

  [TRUMAN *exits*]

NEWTON & MARY & HOWARD We love you in a
  certain way
  And still we'll keep on hoping
  But as long as people need to sugar-coat the truth
  there will always be Capotes
  there will always be Capotes
  Capote, Capote
  Capote at Yaddo
  He came one summer
  and destroyed our lives
  Capote at Yaddo!

[*Blackout on the three of them. Lights up on* NEWTON *sitting all alone with his drink, looking sad. Simultaneous with this speech, lights up on* TRUMAN *standing talking and laughing with someone in dumbshow*]

NEWTON You know, I always imagine those skaters, in the park, twirling in the cold and laughing and I always want to be a part of them and I always feel very sad that I'm not, but if only one time in my fantasy I could lean in and listen to what they're actually laughing and talking about. But, the thing is ...
I don't want to know ... I don't think I ever really want to know ... Let them twirl, let them laugh ... and me, I'll watch and cry, and imagine ...

[*The lights fade on* NEWTON *and* TRUMAN]

[*End*]

Capote at Yaddo

Music

by John Alcorn

To the memory of my brother Peter

Capote at Yaddo

148

153

154

159

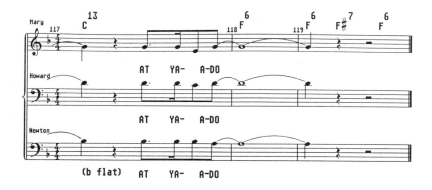

Note: Where required or desired Mary's part may be performed an octave lower than written.

Newton's Song

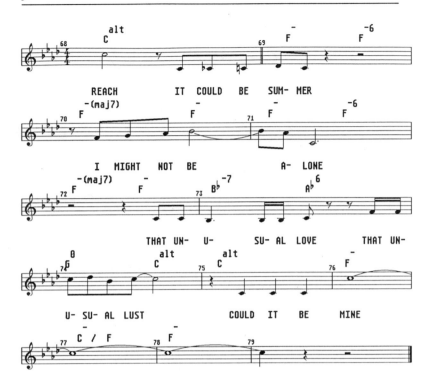

Howard's Song

♩ = 140 swing

HOW MUCH DID HE REAL- LY MEAN TO ME THAT

CHARM- ING BOY OR IS HE JUST THE

UL- TI MATE FUCK IN THE WOODS A KIND OF

WIND UP TOY I MUST BE

RA- TIO- NAL AND SE- PA- RATE THE DARK DONE DEED FROM THE

COLD CLEAR LIGHT OF DAY WELL IF THE

TRUTH BE KNOWN IF ALL IS SAID IT

CER- TAIN- LY WAS DONE I MIGHT AS WELL GIVE HIM A- WAY

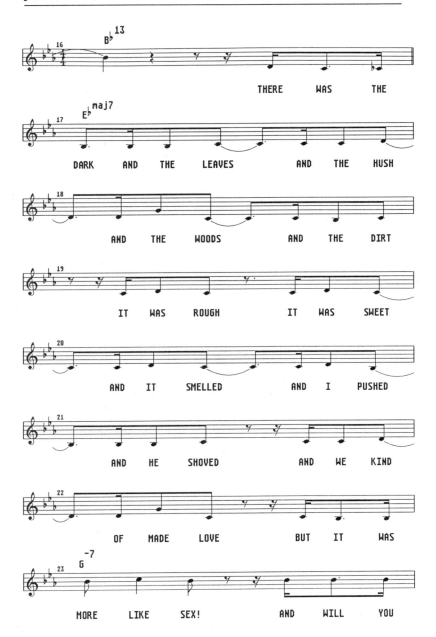

Mary's Song

SO THAT CHARM- ING LIT- TLE VI- PER IS CON- CERNED THAT I

LIKE HIM THERE'S NO REA- SON REAL- LY TO TELL HIM THAT'S A

LIE THERE'S SOME- THING A- BOUT HIM THAT'S RA- THER EN- TER-

TAIN- ING AN AIR OF CHEER- FUL DOOM WHO KNOWS

WHY? OH IT'S NOT EA- SY LOV- ING A NEW- TON AR- VIN ES-

PE- CIAL- LY WHEN HE DOES- N'T LOVE YOU BACK BUT IT'S

HARD- ER STILL WHEN YOUR COM- PE- TI- TION IS A

CUN- NING TWEN- TY YEAR OLD AR- TIS- TIC HACK! I'M IN

LOVE WITH A MAN   WHO DOES-N'T LOVE ME I'M THE

SAND IN HIS EYE   THE FLY IN HIS TEA   IN THE

FLICK OF A HAND HE'D SAY GOOD- BYE   I SHOULD

LEAVE HIM A- LONE   I DON'T KNOW WHY I'M IN

LOVE WITH A MAN   IT'S ALL A LIE   I I-

MA- GINE IT'S GRAND   I MUST OR I'LL CRY WHAT'S

WORST OF ALL   I'VE JUST BEEN HAD   HE'S AS

GAY AS THE DAY   AND I DON'T MEAN GLAD   SO I'VE PRE-

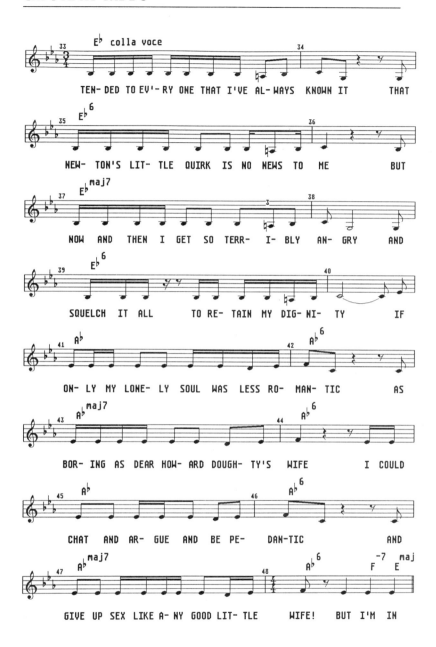

TEN- DED TO EV'- RY ONE THAT I'VE AL- WAYS KNOWN IT   THAT

NEW- TON'S LIT- TLE QUIRK IS NO NEWS TO ME   BUT

NOW AND THEN I GET SO TERR- I- BLY AN- GRY   AND

SQUELCH IT ALL   TO RE- TAIN MY DIG- NI- TY   IF

ON- LY MY LONE- LY SOUL WAS LESS RO- MAN- TIC   AS

BOR- ING AS DEAR HOW- ARD DOUGH- TY'S   WIFE   I COULD

CHAT AND AR- GUE AND BE PE- DAN-TIC   AND

GIVE UP SEX LIKE A- NY GOOD LIT- TLE   WIFE! BUT I'M IN

173

LOVE WITH A MAN WHO LOVES ME NOT IF I

BREAK MY LEG I SHOULD BE SHOT I'M THE

PRICK OF A PIN A GLANCE NOT RE- TURNED A

DREAD- ED COLD THE COF- FEE THAT'S BURNED THE

GRASS THAT'S TOO LONG A DAN- DE- LION PATCH A

FREEZ- ING NORTH WIND AN EGG THAT WON'T HATCH A

TRAIN THAT IS LATE A DOG THAT IS SPAYED A

FUN- GAL IN- FEC- TION AN OP- ER- A- TION DE- LAYED THE

Capote Finale

182

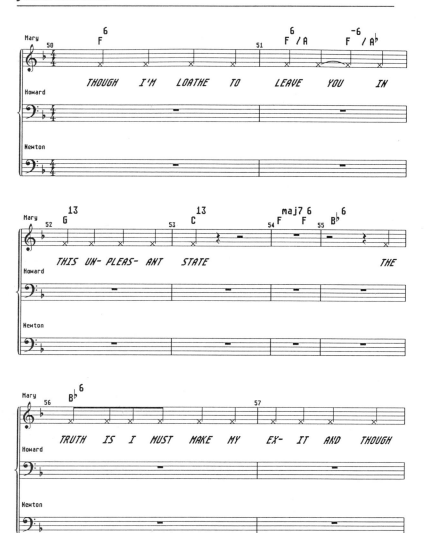

186

187

Note: Where required or desired Mary's part may be performed an octave lower than written.

2-2-Tango

A-Two-Man-One-Man-Show

by Daniel MacIvor

2-2-Tango was first produced by Fringe of Toronto and Great Big Fags (an association between Platform 9 and Da Da Kamera) in Toronto in June 1990 with the following cast:

JAMES, Steve Cumyn
JIM, Daniel MacIvor
YOUTH, Fab Filippo

Director: Ken McDougall
Designer: Ed Roy

The play was remounted by Da Da Kamera and Buddies In Bad Times Theatre in April 1991 with the following cast:

JAMES, Gordon McKerracher
JIM, Daniel MacIvor
YOUTH, Fab Filippo/Adam Nashman

Director: Ken McDougall
Designer: Ed Roy

For permission to perform the play please contact:

Patricia Ney
Christopher Banks and Associates
219 Dufferin Street, Suite 305
Toronto, Canada
M6K 1Y9

Notes:

2-2-Tango is written to be performed in a strictly-choreo-graphed style, both visual and verbal. The dances in the play—Tango, Waltz, Hustle, Charleston—are not meant to be authentic but scaled-down, minimalist versions. When the script calls for the performers to 'sing' it means make a sound (*da, ba, la,* etc.) and sing the basic melody of the dance they are doing.

Unless directed by the script to speak or look at one another, the performers are speaking to the audience.

The set should be a proscenium stage so as to allow quick and clean entrance from and exit to the wings. There should be a feeling of vaudeville. Two identical chairs. There is no need for design to indicate a change of location. We do not change location; we remain onstage.

Both men are attired identically. In the Toronto production the designer selected yellow suits, pink shirts, fluorescent-green ties, black shoes, and round, mirrored sunglasses. Jeans and T-shirts are also a possibility, and budget restraints may require this sort of compromise, but every effort must be made to suggest the men are wearing a 'team' costume. The YOUTH appears in youthful garb (in the original: jeans and a T-shirt).

For John

2-2-Tango

The men begin to sing a tango off-stage. They tango on from opposite sides. They tango off. They tango on carrying watermelons. They tango off. They tango on without watermelons. They notice one another. They stop. JAMES *stage left.* JIM *stage right. They face the audience. A watermelon rolls on and stops in front of* JIM. *A moment of unease.* JIM *rolls it off*

JAMES   First I think it is a feeling of, a recognition that occurs. And this is very personal, this is internal, this is almost independent, yes of the thing that causes it.

   Just that … Just that, image of, yourself, yourself in someone, something, someone else … *your* mind, *your* desire, *your* body … And that's what turns the light on. You see, there you are, standing in the dark, and along comes a light, and the light, although coming from another, is projected entirely on you. And in that light you see yourself, but different, like a mirror, but, a mirror with a mind. And so in the dark you recognize that, light, and then the challenge, to enter the light, to cross the line, to break the ice, to sink or swim away. And then the decision, yes but of course, communication, conversation. 'This, yes, here is a person.' But the question is: just how much like me are they really though? And on the outcome of that judgement rests the inevitability or the improbability of a little warm flesh for the evening.

[*A watermelon rolls in and stops in front of* JAMES. JAMES *rolls it off*]

193

JIM Look I know it's early but it's something I like to get over with early, if that's alright. I mean I wouldn't do like *'Hi'* and hit him with it. No, but, it's better to get it over with from as near to the beginning as possible. If you wait for the middle and it makes things sour then what? You've wasted a whole beginning (and the beginning is the hardest part) and probably a good bit of middle (and the middle can be so nice). So I say, say it and have it done quickly. So …

I must have the light off.

I need the light off.

I have been known to fight to have the light off.

I don't mind a bit of moon, a little street light, I have once or twice agreed to a small candle behind something on the other side of the room. But the light must be off.

And it's not what you're thinking, it's not that at all, it's not that I don't want him seeing me. It's just that I prefer not to see me being seen.

And not only that:

If you can't see it?

It might be … *anything.*

[*The men begin to strike mating poses during the following*]

JAMES V

JIM E

JAMES R

JIM Y

JAMES A

JIM T

JAMES T

JIM R

JAMES A

JIM C

JAMES T

JIM   I

JAMES   V

JIM   E

JAMES & JIM   V - E - R - Y - A - T - T - R - A - C - T - I - V - E
     V - E - R - Y - A - T - T - R - A - C - T - I - V - E
     V - E - R - Y - A - T - T - R - A - C - T - I - V - E
     V - E - R - Y - A - T - T - R - A - C - T - I - V - E
     V - E - R - Y - A - T - T - R - A - C - T - I - V - E
     V - E - R - Y - A - T - T - R - A - C - T - I - V - E
     V - E - R - Y - A - T - T - R - A - C - T - I - V - E

[*They face one another*]

Nice suit.

[*They face out. They sing a Waltz. Their dance brings them close and face-to-face*]

JIM   I like the light off.

JAMES   I hate the dark.

[*They speak to the audience*]

JAMES & JIM   A positive resistance.
This is good.

[*They face one another*]

JIM   There's nothing to be afraid of.

JAMES   Exactly.

[*They speak to the audience*]

JAMES & JIM   Early possibilities:

JAMES   Choose from the following:

JIM   One: orgasm.

JAMES   Two: three,

JIM   four,

195

JAMES & JIM   maybe five nice hours.

JIM   Three: a couple of days.

JAMES & JIM   Or,

JAMES   four: a week.

JAMES & JIM   Choose now.

[*They make the sound of a buzzer*]

Unless ...
there really is such a thing

JAMES   as this thing

JAMES & JIM   this thing that people call

JIM   love.

[*They face one another*]

Jim.

JAMES   James.

JAMES & JIM   Really?
Yes! [*laugh*]
No!
Really?
Yes!

JIM   James?

JAMES   Jim?

JAMES & JIM   Yes!
Oh gee.
Jimmy?
No no no no no no no!

[*They look away. They smile. They look back*]

Well ...

[*They speak to the audience while walking to their chairs*]

JAMES   Now this is something else altogether.

JIM   Here we have
JAMES & JIM   irrational thinking.
JIM   I like you, James.

[JIM *picks up his chair*]

JAMES   I like you, Jim.

[JAMES *picks up his chair. They move their chairs together*]

JIM   So words are spoken spells are cast,
JAMES   and at the centre of everything
JIM   is,
JAMES   'What
JIM   am
JAMES   I
JIM   getting
JAMES   out of it?'

[*They sit*]

And there's nothing wrong with that.
JIM   Nothing.
JAMES   There isn't.
JIM   There's not.
JAMES & JIM   There isn't, there's not.
JAMES   [*to* JIM] There's not.

[*Silence*]

JAMES & JIM   One-two-three-four.

[*They stand. They sing the Hustle*]

Do the Hustle!

[*They do the Hustle*]

JIM   My sister was the skipper on the ship of fools.

197

JAMES   Oh.

JIM   My brother spilt his seed in the gutter.

JAMES   Really.

JIM   My father was a hunchback who made us eat raw meat.

JAMES   Oh.

JIM   My mother once bore a goat.

JAMES   Really.

JAMES & JIM   Do the Hustle!

[*They do the Hustle*]

JIM   My father was a monster.

JAMES   Oh.

JIM   My mother was worse.

JAMES   They beat you?

[JIM *stops doing the Hustle*]

JIM   Wouldn't lay a hand on me.

[JAMES *stops doing the Hustle*]

Wouldn't lay a goddamn hand on me.

JAMES & JIM   Do the Hustle!

[*They do the Hustle.* JIM *takes his seat*]

JAMES   There are no innocent victims. No not one no none no
no there R - N - O - T any. Each actor in the exercise is equally
accountable for the carnage. Once we think of *we* ... (And
I don't know this person—if he should choose to divulge
detailed accounts of his personal life, his childhood, his fears,
his dreams, what is that to me, a stranger? Just stories, just
words) ... but once it is no longer *he* and *I* once it becomes *we*
everything becomes *ours* and innocence exits unnoticed up left
and heads for the bar.

[JIM *exits up left.* JAMES *sings a Jitterbug.* JIM *re-enters with drinks.* JIM *joins the Jitterbug and moves to stand behind* JAMES. JAMES *is not impressed*]

I'm very independent.

JIM   Me too.

JAMES   I savour my independence.

JIM   Me too.

JAMES   And I am attracted by the independence of others.

JIM   Me too.

JAMES   I cannot be relied upon.

JIM   Hey!

[*moves away*] Me neither!

[JAMES *begins the Jitterbug again.* JIM *is silent. Suddenly*]

Catch!

[JIM *runs and leaps into* JAMES*'s arms.* JAMES *does not catch him.* JIM *crashes to the ground*]

Sorry about that.

[JAMES *exits*]

All I'm looking for is a good time. That's all. The only problem is I'm not convinced I've ever even had a good time so what am I supposed to compare the time I'm having to? And the times I thought perhaps I might be starting to feel like I'm having a good time I would drive myself crazy wondering why, and then I would just go back to my normal time, which as far as I can figure is either daylight savings or standard, depending on the season.

[JAMES *re-enters singing a romantic prelude to a Charleston.* JAMES *takes* JIM*'s hand and pulls him to his feet. They Charleston. They finish*]

199

JAMES   Live alone?

JIM   Yeah.
      You?

JAMES   Yeah.

JIM   Yeah?

JAMES   Yeah.
      You?

JIM   Yeah.

JAMES   Yeah?

JIM   Yeah.

   [*They face the audience*]

JAMES & JIM   Just between you and me

JAMES   I'm always certain

JIM   or most times try

JAMES   and am usually successful at

JAMES & JIM   keeping the mess out of my bed.

JAMES   There's the morning to think of

JIM   and the possibility of

JAMES & JIM   an endless and silent breakfast.
      Ideally it's his place

JAMES   with easy access to exits.

JIM   But,

JAMES & JIM   if you take it home,

JIM   there's always the danger

JAMES   that it'll never leave,

JIM   or ...

JAMES   more frightening

JIM   that you won't want

JAMES   it

JIM   to.

   [*They continue to Charleston. They finish facing one another*]

JAMES So.

JIM So.

JAMES Shall we?

JIM Sure.

[*They turn and exit in opposite directions. They re-enter*]

JAMES & JIM Where are you going?
   Your place.
   What's wrong with your place?

[JIM *turns facing off.* JAMES *speaks to the audience*]

JAMES Well someone has to make the sacrifice. When it comes
   down to it. I'll take him home and if he won't leave ... I'll kill
   him.
   Just kidding.
   Really.

[JAMES *takes a position behind* JIM]

   Ready?

JIM Ready.

JAMES One

JIM Two

JAMES Three

JIM Four.

JAMES One

JIM Two

JAMES Three

JIM Four.

JAMES & JIM One two three four.
   One two three four.
   One two three four.
   One two three four.

JAMES It takes

JIM two to.

JAMES & JIM One two three four.
One two three four.

JIM Two to.

JAMES One two.

JAMES & JIM Two two three four.

JAMES It takes two to.

[*Beat*]

JAMES & JIM It takes two to.

[*Beat*]

Two two two two two two three four.
Two two two two two two three four.

JAMES Two two two two two two three four.
Two two two two two two three four.

JIM [*simultaneously*] It takes two to taaaaaaaang-*oh!*
It takes two to taaaaaaaang-*oh!*

JAMES It takes one two.

[*Beat*]

JIM It takes two to.

[*Beat*]

JAMES & JIM It takes one two it takes two to.
It takes one two it takes two to.

JAMES One two.

JIM Two to.

JAMES One two.

JIM Two to.

JAMES One two.

JIM Two to.

JAMES & JIM To taaaaaang-*oh!*

Gordon McKerracher (JAMES) and Daniel MacIvor (JIM)
Photographer: Dina Almeida

To taaaaaang-*oh!*
It takes two to taaaaaang-*oh!*
It takes two to taaaaaang-*oh!*
It takes two two two two
two two two two
two two two two
two two two tang to tang
to tang
to tang
to tang
oh! oh! oh! oh!

JAMES This
JIM is not
JAMES This
JIM is not
JAMES This
JIM is not
JAMES This
JIM is not
JAMES a tang
JIM *go!*
JAMES though.

JAMES & JIM [*as they exit*] This is not a tango though, this is not a tango though, this is not a tango though … [*repeat*]

[*They exit. Then re-enter repeating double time as they cross to other exit*] This is not a tango though, this is not a tango though, this is not a tango though … [*repeat*]

[*Black. In the black* JIM *enters and stands centre.* JAMES *enters behind him, a clip-light on his arm. This light is the lighting source*]

JIM If I'm standing by the stereo checking out his CD's and he should come up behind me ...

[JAMES *puts his arm around* JIM, *illuminating his face*]

And if he might then in this position put his feet on either side of mine and put his lips on that spot at the back of my neck and start kissing and the kisses turn to little bites ...

[JIM *turns off the light. In the black*]

... and the bites become bigger. Well if he's into it I'm into a bit of it. Or if my arms should get pinned above my head in the bed later on ...

[JAMES *turns on the light.* JIM, *eyes closed, does not notice*]

... if he likes that I can like it too.
I'm a flexible guy, I'm a flexible man, I'm a flexible guy. French, Greek, B & D, S & M, a water sport now and then, a scattering of humiliation, him hanging from his ankles in the centre of the room with a snake around his body ...
I don't mind that.

[JIM *opens his eyes into the light*]

But the light must always be off.

[JIM *turns the light off.* JAMES *turns the light on.* JIM *turns the light off.* JAMES *turns the light on.* JIM *sulks.* JAMES *moves to turn off the light.* JIM *smiles. Black. In the black: rhythmic sex sounds from the men. These sounds build to a climax of three sustained notes and then ...*]

JAMES & JIM   JIIIIMMMMMIIIIEEEE!

[*Both men light cigarettes. Black. In the black*]

JIM   It's raining out.
JAMES   Yeah.

205

JIM I love the sound of rain.

JAMES Yeah.

JIM It's nice isn't it.

JAMES Yeah.

JIM Can you hear it?

JAMES No.

JIM Neither can I.
I can almost imagine it though.
Can you?

JAMES Yeah.

JIM Shh. Listen.

[*Pause*]

It's nice isn't it.

JAMES Yeah.

JIM [*illuminates his face with his cigarette lighter*] But I don't like any of this stillness business, none of this stillness business and studying one another's face like some goddamn Van Gogh, gazing into one another's eyes like an optician, checking out his body like you're thinking of giving him a tattoo. I like movement, activity and the pursuit of the orgasm at all times. I like to save my thinking for my moments alone. Thinking is for the toilet. The bedroom is the home of fierce action only.

[JIM *light out.* JAMES *light on*]

JAMES Responsibility, yes, responsibility is a word, responsibility is a word one might use, I wouldn't, one might, I certainly wouldn't, one might, though, personally myself, me, I, I … and have you ever noticed how many *I*'s in the word responsibility? Make of it what you will but personally, for me, the word responsibility sits in my stomach like a grapefruit-sized cancer. So it is not a word I would use. Unless of course I was talking about someone else.

206

[JAMES *light out.* JIM *light on*]

JIM   And if by some chance I should happen to fall asleep I don't want any of this 'a roll in the morning,' thank you plainly no. It's just not my style okay. I'm not trying to make it an issue, I'm just saying it to get it said. There are things I will and will not do but more often than not I'm a flexible guy. I'm a flexible guy but not in the morning.

[JIM *light out.* JAMES *light on*]

JAMES   I have heard talk I suppose of Altruism. Uh-hm. It's possible, it's entirely possible, anything's possible. Myself however? It and I remain strangers. If *you* though should happen to meet it though—some party … some street corner—do please do please do insist that it give me a 'ding.'

[JAMES *light out. Pause.* JAMES *and* JIM *light on. They slowly look at one another. Lights out*]

JAMES & JIM   Frightening Possibility Number One.

[*Stage light up full.* JAMES *and* JIM *sitting.* JAMES *smiles at* JIM. JIM *blushes and looks away.* JAMES *takes out a knife and stabs* JIM. JIM *dies. Black*]

Frightening Possibility Number Two.

[*Stage light up full.* JAMES *and* JIM *hum a sappy love song to one another. They kiss their fingers and reach across the space to touch each other's lips. Black*]

Frightening Possibility Number Three.

[*Light up*]

How do you think that makes me feel?
What do you want me to do about it?

Can't you hear what I'm saying?
Who do you think you are?
How long is this going to go on?
Are you serious?
Is this what you want?
Why do you always do that?
What do I do?
Is that all?
You tell me!

[*Beat*]

It's not that I'm not happy it's just I don't think that you are.

[*Black*]

Frightening Possibility Number Four.

[*Light up.* JIM *weeps. Black*]

Frightening Possibility Number Five.

[*Light up.* JAMES *and* JIM *weep. Black*]

Frightening Possibility Number Six.

[*Light up*]

JAMES Fluffy.
JIM Terrance.
JAMES Zorro.
JIM Felix.
JAMES & JIM Whiskers!

[*Beat*]

Nah.
JAMES Nietzsche.
JIM Pussy.

JAMES Debby.

JIM Hamlet.

JAMES & JIM Whiskers!
    I said that!

[*Black*]

    Frightening Possibility Number Seven.

[*Light up.* JAMES *and* JIM *yawn. They look at one another and give a little smile. They look away and roll their eyes. Black*]

    Frightening Possibility Number Eight.

[*Light up.* JAMES *and* JIM *stand together.* JIM *holds a watermelon wrapped in a pink baby-blanket. They pose as if for a portrait. Black*]

    Frightening Possibility Number Nine.

[*Light up.* JIM *stands behind the sitting* JAMES]

JIM [*in a funny voice*] Are you gumpy today? Don't be gumpy baybee. What for are you gumpy Mister Serious. Don't be gumpy. Mister Serious Gumpy. Gumpy gumpy baybee. Don't be gumpy.

[*Black*]

JAMES & JIM Frightening Possibility Number Ten.

[*Light up*]

JAMES Please don't.

JIM Don't what?

JAMES That voice.

JIM What voice?

JAMES That voice you were doing.

JIM I wasn't 'doing' a voice.

JAMES Well you were making a voice, talking in a voice.

JIM Was I?

JAMES You know that you were and if you do it again …

JIM What? What? Get really violent? Rip out my vocal chords?

JAMES Just don't.

JIM It's my voice to do with what I please.

JAMES Well you wouldn't do it if you knew how fucking stupid it sounded.

[JIM *pulls out a knife and stabs* JAMES. JAMES *dies*]

JIM Mister Gumpy go bye bye.

[*Black. Slow fade-up lights*]

One-two-three-four. [*looks at* JAMES]
One-two-three-four. [*looks at* JAMES]
This is a dance!

[JAMES *steps forward independently*]

One-two-three-four!

JAMES This is a dance.

JIM One-two-three-four!

JAMES This is a dance.

JIM One-two-three-four!

JAMES This is a dance.

JIM One-two-three-four!

JAMES This is an indepen dance.

[JIM *steps forward and stands parallel to* JAMES]

JIM This is an indepen dance.

JAMES & JIM This is an indepen
    indepen
    indepen dance.

JAMES This is an

    indepen
    indepen
    indepen
    indepen dance.

JIM   [*simultaneously*] Dance dance
    dance dance
    dance dance
    dance dance.

JAMES & JIM   This is a dance.

    [*Pause*]

    Dance dance
    dance dance.
    This is a dance.
    This is a dance.
    This is a dance.
    This is a dance.
    This is a dance.
    This is a dance.
    This is an indepen dance.
    This is an indepen dance.
    This is an indepen dance.

JAMES   This is an indepen

JIM   indepen

JAMES & JIM   This is an indepen dance.

JIM   Hands in your pockets.

JAMES & JIM   Dance dance.

JAMES   Eyes on the door.

JAMES & JIM   Dance dance.

JIM   Head on your shoulders.

JAMES & JIM   Dance dance.

JAMES   Feet on the floor hands in your pockets.

JIM   Eyes on the door.

JAMES   Head on your shoulders.

JIM   Feet on the floor.

JAMES & JIM   This is a dance.

[*Beat*]

JAMES   This is a dance dance
   dance dance
   dance dance
   dance dance.

JIM   [*simultaneously*] This is a
   dance dance
   dance dance.

JAMES & JIM   This is an indepen dance.
   This is an indepen dance.
   Can only be done:
   Can only be done:
   Can only be done can only be done can only be done:

JAMES   Alone.

JIM   Can only be done:

JAMES   Alone.

JAMES & JIM   Can only be done can only be done can only be done:

JIM   With me.

JAMES   Can only be done:

JIM   With me.

JAMES & JIM   Can only be done can only be done can only be done:

JIM   With me.

JAMES   Alone.

JIM   With me.

JAMES   Alone.

[*They repeat these final two lines twenty times, then they both
draw knives and face one another. The line repetition becomes
frenetic. Then a watermelon smashes to the floor between them.*]

They regard the watermelon as light fades. Light up. JAMES *sits facing out.* JIM *sits facing* JAMES]

So.

JIM Yeah.

JAMES Well.

JIM So.

JAMES Then.

JIM Well.

JAMES Uh ...

JIM Good hands, car keys, tennis balls, bicycle paths, beer, dark wood, shovels, sand, the smell of a shaving brush, wrestling, neckties, cigars, dirty socks, newspapers, bad jokes, late nights, good hands?

JAMES No thank you.

JIM [*turns out*] I didn't think so.

JAMES But thank you.

JIM So.

JAMES Then.

JIM Well.

JAMES So.

JIM Then.

JAMES Well.

[*They stand*]

JAMES & JIM Ciao.

[*They begin to exit in opposite directions. They stop.* JIM *looks out to the audience*]

JIM In this dream I wake up in the morning and there is a boy in my room and he is offering me watermelon and at first I think how much I would like a slice of watermelon so I take it and then I ask the boy to dance and while we are dancing he is looking out the window and not saying anything and so I stop and ask the boy, 'Don't you like to dance?' and he asks me if he might use my telephone and while he is on the telephone I realize that this watermelon is a burden to him and he was just trying to get rid of it and he was friendly to me only because he finds me pathetic and when he's finished on the telephone he picks up his tray of watermelon and he leaves and I watch him from my window as he walks through the neighbourhood checking the numbers of the houses against something he wrote on a piece of paper while he was on the telephone and then I go back to bed, and then I wake up, and when I wake up I don't feel sad. I just feel … normal.

[JIM *looks away.* JAMES *looks out to the audience*]

JAMES   In this dream I am standing on a dirt road and a boy approaches and offers me a slice of watermelon from a tray he carries and I take the tray from him and I put it on the ground and I take the boy's face in my hands and I kiss him and while I am kissing him the sun dries out the watermelon and when the boy notices this he begins to cry and I feel bad for a moment and then I walk away, I do not eat any of the watermelon even though it seems this would make the boy feel better, I just feel bad for the boy for a moment and then I walk away and as I am walking I think that I should have taken a slice of the watermelon anyway, I could have thrown it away later but then something else catches my eye … and I forget about the boy.

[*They exit to opposite sides. Black. Light up*]

JAMES & JIM   [*off-stage*] Epilogue!

[*They enter and take up positions on opposite sides of the stage. They wear dark glasses and speak to the audience*]

It's sometime later.

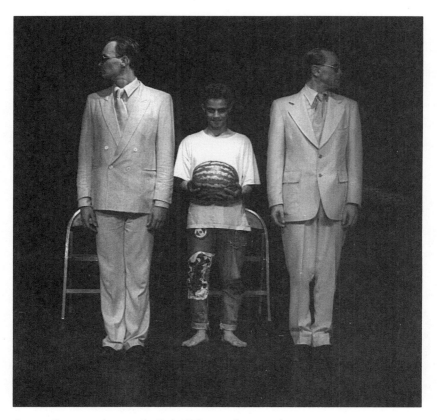

Steve Cumyn (JAMES), Fab Filippo (YOUTH),
and Daniel MacIvor (JIM)
Photographer: Lisa Walter

JAMES And I was there
JIM you know
JAMES and I was looking at something.
JIM Nothing really.
JAMES & JIM Waiting really.
JAMES Just waiting.
JIM Not really looking
JAMES & JIM at anything.

215

JAMES And you were

JIM you were

JAMES & JIM way over there on the other side.

JAMES You had your hip stuck out

JAMES & JIM leaning

JIM and one hand—

JAMES & JIM not posed—

JAMES casually placed on your hip.

JAMES & JIM Like this.

JIM And I watched you

JAMES for a long time

JIM and I became

JAMES & JIM so satisfied.

'I've had him,' I was thinking.

JAMES And you looked up

JIM over

JAMES & JIM saw me,

JAMES and the look on my face

JIM or the feeling in the air

JAMES & JIM and you mouthed:

[*They mouth 'Fuck off'*]

JAMES I was saddened when you turned and walked away.

JAMES & JIM But when I saw

JIM. how your ass

JAMES moved

JIM back and

JAMES forth a-

JIM gainst the

JAMES swing-

JIM ing

JAMES of

JIM your

JAMES   arms,
JIM   I realized

[*They look at one another*]

JAMES & JIM   I had mistaken you for someone else.

[JAMES *and* JIM *facing out begin independently repeating their mating actions. We hear a dance-club-type song. A beautiful boy enters carrying a tray of sliced watermelon. The boy offers a slice to* JIM. *He does not notice the boy. The boy offers a slice to* JAMES. *He does not notice the boy but takes a slice of watermelon and devours it hungrily. The boy places the tray at the front of the stage and indicates it as an offering to the audience. The boy takes a position up centre. Smiles. Black*]

[*End*]

Brave Hearts

by Harry Rintoul

Brave Hearts was first produced by Buddies In Bad Times Theatre in Toronto in April 1991 with the following cast:

G.W., Murray Oliver
RAFE, Ted Atherton

Director: Bryden MacDonald
Lighting Designer: Jan Elliott
Stage Manager: Deborah Ratelle
Artistic Director: Sky Gilbert

Brave Hearts was originally workshopped through the Manitoba Association of Playwrights, Playwrights Development Program in June 1990 with the following cast:

G.W., Brian Drader
RAFE, Jonathan Barrett

Director: Doug Arrell
Stage Manager: Kelly Wilson

For permission to perform the play please contact:

The Manitoba Association of Playwrights
503-100 Arthur Street
Winnipeg, Canada
R3B 1H3

Characters:

G.W., twenty-five years old. A loner with a sense of humour. He works on a ranch raising horses. He has a working-man look.

RAFE, thirty-one years old. A guilt-ridden alcoholic. He's far too hard on himself, takes everything personally, and seems beaten down by the world around him. He wears designer jeans and a polo shirt.

Setting:

The play takes place in the present, on a Saturday evening in August, around the picnic table in the backyard of an acreage outside the city of Saskatoon, Saskatchewan.

Notes:

Lighting is simple. Lights up, lights down. If possible, the light should fade slowly during the play. The effect should be of nightfall.

Certain lines of dialogue are stepped on by the preceeding or following line. This is indicated in the text by the direction *overlapping*. Care should be taken that, while lines are said fast and are overlapping, the effect of the line is not lost, and the lines are still heard clearly.

The 'butchering' of RAFE's favourite song, 'Wichita Lineman,' refers to the words that G.W. sings. It is important that the words he sings not be the correct ones.

It is considered an insult to refer to a rancher (anyone who raises cattle or horses) as a 'farmer' as RAFE does.

When G.W. exits to the house, there should be music coming from the party inside the house. Music should be party music, rock 'n' roll, some country. No club music.

There are two pieces of music that should be used in production. For the opening of the show, 'Everytime I Think of You' by The Babies, and for the closing, 'Wichita Lineman' by Glen Campbell.

I would be true for there are those who trust me
I would be pure for there are those who care,
I would be strong for there is much to suffer,
I would be brave for there is much to dare.

— H.A. WALTER

For Dave

Brave Hearts

As the lights come up, G.W. *is sitting on top of the picnic table,*
holding a beer in his hands, staring out at the prairie, looking at
nothing in particular, tapping his feet in time with a Dwight
Yoakam tape playing off-stage. He takes off his hat, sets it on the
table, yawns, stretches, lies back on the table. He tries balancing
the beer on his forehead, almost spills it, and then sets it on the
table. For a while he stares at the sky, then sits up, puts his hat on
backwards, looks around, shakes his head, sighs, and takes a long
sip of his beer. Off-stage, the tape abruptly stops and the sound
of smashing glass is heard

G.W. Aw geez, what now?

[G.W. *sets his beer on the ground under the table. He crosses*
towards the house and bumps into RAFE *as he comes storming*
out of the house. RAFE *sits down at the picnic table.* G.W. *stops*
for a moment, takes a long look at RAFE, *smiles, then exits into*
the house. RAFE *gets up, paces around the picnic table. He kicks*
a half-empty beer case off the bench of the picnic table into the
nearby field and paces]

RAFE Fuck.

[*He paces, then stops, smashing the top of the table with his fists*]

Fuck. Fuck. Fuck.

[*He turns towards the house*]

Fuck.

[*He kicks at the picnic table, then stops, sits down, takes several deep breaths*]

Real cool move Rafe, real smart ... fuck. God damn it all anyways.

[*He gets up, walks around the table. As he's walking he notices* G.W.*'s beer, picks it up, rolls it between the palms of his hands, thinks about drinking it, decides not to, and puts it back. He sits down, takes a long, deep breath, shakes his head, drops it into his hands, and runs his hand through his hair as he looks towards the house*]

[*shouting*] Fucking faggot.

[*He snaps his head back, stretching his arms and his legs out as far as they will go, tensing his whole body, then instantly collapsing it. He sits, rubs his hands, takes several deep breaths.* G.W. *enters, his cap still on backwards, carrying a beer in each hand*]

Now we go to motorcade, pride of pookas on parade ...
G.W. Safe to come out here?
RAFE You fuckin' figure it out.
G.W. You okay?

[RAFE *does not respond*]

Hello? Anybody in there? It's Rafe, isn't it?
RAFE What the hell do you want?
G.W. Just thought I'd come out and see how you were that's all.

[RAFE *does not respond*]

Brought you a beer.

[*He dangles the beer, then sets it on the table, sets his own down, picks up the beer off the ground*]

Seems kind of unfair if you think about it.

[RAFE *does not respond*]

   Danny's got a whole crowd of people looking after him and you're out here all alone.

RAFE I was.

G.W. [*sitting on top of the table*] Course you're as popular as a half hour of dry heaves right now, so I guess that explains that.

RAFE What are you doing out here?

G.W. Like I said I came out to see how you were.

RAFE Yeah well I don't need a baby-sitter so piss off.

G.W. That's up to you.

RAFE You got that right.

G.W. Well good for me then.

RAFE If you say so.

   [*Pause*]

G.W. So ... come here often?

RAFE Why don't you just fuck off.

G.W. Can't.

RAFE Why not?

G.W. Dibs.

RAFE What dibs?

G.W. You know you've really screwed things up here. I mean I doubt if I can have a good time now.

RAFE Then there's no reason for you to stay so fuck off.

G.W. Like I said, if you were listening, I've got dibs.

RAFE On what?

G.W. The picnic table.

RAFE The picnic table?

G.W. Yeah. Any time Jimmy asks me to attend one of his little get-togethers, I tell him if he guarantees I don't have to talk to anyone, see anyone or have anything to do with anything going on, I'll show up. In return I get to have my own kind of fun, which is sitting out here on the picnic table enjoying the wonders of Mother Nature. And now you've ruined it.

RAFE Well you can still sit out here, keep your mouth shut and you won't know I'm here.

G.W. It's not quite the same thing.

RAFE Tough.

G.W. It won't work like this, trust me.

RAFE Then I guess you'll just have to try and adjust.

G.W. I like to be alone. Okay? By myself.

RAFE You mean you come to a party to sit in the backyard by yourself?

G.W. Hey whoa. Since when do I owe you an explanation. I mean I haven't asked you if the only reason you showed up here tonight was to get into an argument with Danny and then punch him in the face. All I've done is come out to see if you're okay.

RAFE Well I'm fine, so you can bugger off.

G.W. Stupid me. I thought you might feel some remorse after ploughing him in the face.

RAFE He had it coming.

G.W. He did not.

RAFE He's a fuckin' faggot.

[*Pause.* RAFE *starts to exit*]

G.W. Where do you think you're going?

RAFE I'm getting out of here.

G.W. You can't leave.

RAFE Watch me.

G.W. I wouldn't if I were you.

RAFE You're not me.

G.W. You'll have to go through the house.

RAFE Yeah so?

G.W. Everyone's pretty upset about what you did to Danny.

RAFE So they're upset, so what?

G.W. They're really mad.

RAFE So am I.

G.W. Truth is they're really quite angry, and Tony, he's a lawyer, he's up on his high horse ranting an' raving about how Jimmy and Danny should sue you.

RAFE He sounds like a fucking ambulance-chaser.

G.W. What did Shakespeare say? The first thing we do is kill all the lawyers. Henry Four, I believe, or is it Henry Four Part Two.

RAFE Henry Six. Part Two.

G.W. Oh. Anyways, Tony, who I will admit is a shyster, and, as you so aptly put it, a fucking ambulance-chaser, has everyone really worked up.

RAFE It's none of his business.

G.W. You don't get it. Tony can really work a crowd. Everyone's angry.

RAFE I'll apologize to Danny, to Jimmy, and it'll be okay.

G.W. Apologizing isn't going to be enough.

RAFE I'll talk to Jimmy, I'll explain to him.

G.W. He's angry 'cause you made a mess of the place.

RAFE What mess?

G.W. There's blood everywhere.

RAFE What blood? I only hit him once.

G.W. Then there's all the broken glass.

RAFE What are you talking about? What broken glass?

G.W. From when you hit Danny.

RAFE I hit him with my fist not a goddamn beer bottle. What are you talking about blood and broken glass?

G.W. You punched him, he tripped over Jimmy's cat, landing face down on top of the glass coffee table which shattered beneath him ...

RAFE What? What the hell ... Is he okay?

G.W. For someone who had it coming, he's fine.

RAFE Oh shit. Shit, shit, shit.

G.W. It's not bad, not really too bad at all, he's got a couple of cuts.

RAFE Oh shit.

G.W. It's nothing serious, I mean he's not gonna need stitches or anything like that, Jerry's patching him up, he's a doctor, well actually he's a vet, but—

RAFE Shit, shit, shit

G.W. Really really, he's fine, he'll be okay ... Now where are you going?

RAFE I should go see if he's okay.

G.W. You can't. It's not as bad as it sounds, you know how Jimmy exaggerates things, there's some blood and some glass but it's not real bad, it's just everyone is really angry with you and it's better if you let them calm down. You don't know these guys. If you walk in there now it'd be like throwing gasoline on a fire, everything'd just erupt, you know? ... It'd just upset everyone.

RAFE I didn't mean for that to happen ... I didn't mean for him to land on the coffee table ... for that to happen.

[*He takes a step towards the house*]

I wanna tell him that.

[**G.W.** *steps in front of* **RAFE**, *blocking his way*]

G.W. Give it some time, sit down, relax, let everyone cool down a bit. I mean they're a tight little bunch—

RAFE Maybe you're right.

G.W. I've been right before, anyways, later, if you want to, once everyone's cooled down, you can go in.

RAFE Fuck.

G.W. Take it easy, I told you it's not serious.

RAFE I wanna see how he is.

G.W. Why? He's just—what were your exact words—a fuckin' faggot? You got a real ear for alliteration, know that?

RAFE Why don't you shut the fuck up?

G.W. You sure do swear a great deal for a person your age.

RAFE What the fuck … What's that got to do with anything?

G.W. You swear a lot. You use profanity.

RAFE And I suppose you don't swear?

G.W. Sometimes. I think you do it to draw attention to yourself, or you're very insecure, or you have a poor vocabulary.

RAFE I'm going to see Danny.

G.W. You go in there, they're going to beat the crap out of you. Danny is everyone's friend. They all like Danny and they don't like what you did. Kenny's really mad. It's everything they can do to keep him from coming out here after you. Kenny boxed pro for three years. You want my honest opinion—I don't think you'd last too long. Look, if you just sit down, relax a little, everything's gonna blow over, and in a while, it'll be like nothing happened.

[RAFE *looks at him, looks to the house*]

You wanna go in there, go, but I don't fight so it would be you against them.

[*pause*] Besides, you're driving the blue Chevy half-ton with the Silver Stirrup running boards and the powder-blue two-tone topper aren't you?

RAFE Yeah.

G.W. You got a problem.

RAFE How so?

G.W. Danny's Buick is parked on your driver's side. On the passenger side you've got Kenny's Jeep. Now, it's just my opinion, but right now if you asked them to move, I don't think they would. And then you're parked right up against the garage door. Couldn't back up if you wanted to because parked right behind you, hugging your ass-end, you've got a beat-up Ford. That's mine. And right now I don't feel like moving it.

RAFE Fine. Fine. If I can't fucking leave, then I guess I gotta sit here until I can.

G.W. Good, just sit down, everything'll blow over, and to pass the time, you can tell me your life story. Drink your beer.

RAFE I don't drink.

G.W. Okay then I'll drink it.

RAFE [overlapping] Who told you I drink? Jimmy? Jimmy tell you that?

G.W. [overlapping] It's just a beer ...

RAFE [resentful towards Jimmy] He knows damn well I don't drink, I've told him a thousand times, but I'm not one step in the door and he hands me a vodka. Drink this Rafe, Rafe loosen up, lighten up, join the party.

G.W. He wants everyone to have a good time, that's his nature. It's a little nauseating at times I'll grant you that.

RAFE [overlapping. Jokingly] I poured the vodka into the plant. He brought me another one, I poured it into the plant. When the plant was waterlogged I started pouring them into the cat's dish.

G.W. That would explain why Tippy was passed out.

RAFE He caught me doing that, then he wouldn't talk to me. So I just sat there. Everyone was standing around, no one else would talk to me after Jimmy reamed me out for getting the cat bombed, I got up to look at the tapes and then that little faggot ...

G.W. Why did you come here tonight?

RAFE What are you, a cop?

G.W. No, I mean I just find it a little strange that you keep referring to Danny as that little faggot ...

RAFE I hate the little shit.

G.W. I don't think you're one of his favourite people either.

RAFE He's irritating.

G.W. He's nineteen. Granted he's not the most mature nineteen-year-old you'll ever meet.

RAFE He whines.

G.W. Oh well let's have him killed. But then you've already tried that.

RAFE What is your fucking problem?

G.W. I'm not the one with the problem.

RAFE Why are you sticking up for him?

G.W. Because I don't think people should be hit in the face. All you would have had to do is tell him to cool it but—

RAFE I told him to back off and he didn't.

G.W. You still didn't have to paste him one.

RAFE So I'm the one in the wrong? I'm the bad guy.

G.W. I never said that.

RAFE You sure as hell did.

G.W. Listen up. What I said was you both behaved like idiots. Okay? Danny was wrong. You were wrong.

RAFE So what should I do? Get myself a rope and hang myself from the nearest tree?

G.W. Why are you getting yourself all worked up? It was an accident, a misunderstanding that shouldn't have happened. It would have been better if it hadn't but it did. Shit happens. There, I swore. See? Sometimes I do swear.

RAFE Shit happens. That's all you have to say? Shit happens.

G.W. Whether you want it to or not.

RAFE And you're saying nobody'll think the worse of me for what happened tonight?

G.W. I wouldn't ask Danny to donate a kidney if you ever need one.

RAFE And what about me? What about how I feel about it?

G.W. I don't know how you feel about it. All you've done so far is blame everything that's happened on Danny.

RAFE I'm offended. Okay? I'm fucking offended. I don't like what happened. I don't know Danny. I've seen him around, all I know is he's a friend of Jimmy's. I've never met him, we've never even been introduced so what right has he to walk up to me, cup his hand, slap it against my crotch, hold it there and whine, 'Ooohh this feels good, where you been all my life, lover?' Where does he get off doin' that to me? What right has he got to do that?

G.W. None. None at all.

RAFE You got that right.

G.W. He acted on impulse, he was a little loaded.

RAFE Bein' a little loaded is no excuse.

G.W. He screwed up. You could cut him some slack.

RAFE He's a little faggot.

G.W. Why the hell are you here?

RAFE I was invited.

G.W. That doesn't answer the question.

RAFE Maybe it's none of your business.

G.W. You hate faggots. That's what you said. Isn't that what you said?

RAFE You don't know what I mean when I say—

G.W. [overlapping] It's a fag party. Everyone of us is a fag. Jimmy, Danny, Kenny, Jerry, Tommy, Tony, Terry—sounds like a kindergarten class doesn't it? So what were you expecting? Why'd you bother to come tonight if you hate faggots so much?

RAFE I was invited.

G.W. That's an excuse, it's not an answer.

RAFE I didn't have anything else to do so I thought I'd—

G.W. Come and punch out a faggot.

RAFE I didn't mean ... When I said faggot, I didn't mean to imply—

G.W. That you hate faggots.

RAFE Danny is the kind of—

G.W. Faggot.

RAFE He's the kind I don't like.

G.W. I never would have guessed.

RAFE Fuck you, you don't wanna listen.

G.W. I don't have to listen. I've heard it all before, guys like you.

RAFE What? Guys like me what?

G.W. Guys like you give guys like me a bad name.

RAFE I don't mean to say that you're—

G.W. [*overlapping*] I don't think you know what you mean.

RAFE You're not like Danny.

G.W. Yes I am.

RAFE Danny's the kind of—

G.W. [*guessing*] Oh, uh, faggot.

RAFE Are you gonna listen or not?

G.W. Hey. I'm all ears.

RAFE I don't like Danny because he's always prancing ... always primping, prissing, preening, posing, and that goddamned lisp of his. Guys like him—the ones that work as aestheticians in the beauty salons in the malls, the ones that wear their make-up, posing all the time—guys like that make me sick. That's what I mean when I call him a faggot.

G.W. So you punch them in the mouth, a real rational way of dealing with the situation. Ever hear of live and let live?

RAFE I told him to back off, but he wouldn't. Fuck it, I should have stayed home.

G.W. But you didn't and look at the fun we're having now.

RAFE Some fun.

[RAFE *gets up and starts pacing. He paces upstage, turns on one step, then paces downstage*]

G.W. Why don't you drink your beer—

RAFE [*overlapping*] I told you.

G.W. Or don't drink it.

235

RAFE What a fucking mess. I don't believe this. Fucking pipe dream.

G.W. What is?

RAFE What did I come here for?

G.W. It beats watching Donahue. Actually Donahue's gotten kind of boring lately. Have you noticed that? I mean even Geraldo isn't worth watching anymore.

RAFE Nothing changes, nothing gets any better, it's the same thing every time, over and over again.

G.W. Actually I think talk-TV is finished, how about you?

RAFE Why do I do this to myself? Why? Geezus you'd think I would have learned by now.

G.W. Oh for crying out loud lighten up! Sit down and relax. It's not the end of the world. We all make mistakes so don't be so hard on yourself. Things'll work themselves out.

RAFE The last thing I need from you is a bunch of cute-assed clichés that are supposed to make me feel better.

G.W. You know there's a term for what you're doing, it's a behavioural thing, caged animals in zoos do it. You're doing it. You know you're taking exactly eight paces in one direction, turning with one step, then taking eight paces in the other direction. Feeling trapped Rafe? A little caged?

RAFE No. No I'm not.

G.W. So can I ask you something?

RAFE Will you shut up after that?

G.W. Sure.

RAFE So?

G.W. Why did you come here tonight?

RAFE Give it a fucking break.

G.W. You said I could ask.

RAFE Just sit there and shut the hell up.

[RAFE *stands looking at the prairie.* G.W. *sips his beer, looks*

236

around, looks to the house, looks at RAFE *and smiles. Pause.* G.W. *starts to sing the first line of 'Wichita Lineman,' getting the words wrong]*

RAFE No singing.

G.W. You don't like Glen Campbell? How can anyone not like Glen Campbell?

RAFE I like Glen Campbell, I do. What I don't like is listening to you butcher one of my favourite songs.

G.W. It's amazing.

RAFE What? That you can't sing?

G.W. That out of the thousands of songs there are I chose to sing your favourite song. Do you have any idea what the mathematical odds against such an event are?

RAFE No.

G.W. Any requests?

RAFE Yeah. Shut up. [*he starts pacing*]

G.W. I wonder why more people don't like country music. I mean thematically it has everything that anyone could want. Love. Pain. Anguish and heartache.

[G.W. *starts to sing 'Stand by Your Man.'* RAFE *turns on* G.W., *looks at him*]

Alcoholism. Drug addiction. Lost loves. Found loves. Jail. Trucks. Dogs. Kids. God. Mothers who love their truck-driving sons, sons who love their truck-driving mothers. Loneliness. [*he starts to sing 'Sleeping Single in a Double Bed'*] ... or is it sleeping double in a single bed? That doesn't make much sense, wouldn't be very comfortable either. I mean it's chock-full of just good, old-fashioned misery.

RAFE You're not gonna shut up are you?

G.W. Probably not. Why don't you relax?

RAFE I don't feel like relaxing.

G.W. Then sit down, you're gonna create a trail. It's not good for the grass.

RAFE I sit all day, I like being on my feet.

[*Pause*]

G.W. [*looks at the sky*] Look. Look at that.

RAFE What is it— Kenny?

G.W. It's not Kenny, it's a cloud.

RAFE Great. [*looking*] It's just a cloud.

G.W. It's not just a cloud, it's a grey one, dark and rich with rain deep inside, billowing and rolling, building, alive, pulsing ...

RAFE Don't hold your breath.

G.W. [*angrily*] You could think about someone else for a change.

RAFE What the fuck did I do now?

G.W. Some of us want it to rain. Some of us need rain. Dugouts are all dried up, pasture's shot, grass's dead, what isn't burnt to a crisp just blows away.

RAFE Things are pretty bad.

G.W. There's nothing pretty about it.

RAFE It's a farmer's life—always praying for something ...

G.W. I'm not a farmer.

RAFE Oh, then what do you do?

G.W. I raise horses.

RAFE Really?

G.W. Such exclamation in your tone, surprise in your voice. You didn't think fags raised horses?

RAFE I never said that.

G.W. I raise horses, so what?

RAFE So that's okay.

G.W. Meets with your approval does it?

RAFE All I did was ask you what you do.

G.W. And I just told you.

RAFE So now you can shut up.

G.W. So what do you do when you're not punching people out?

RAFE Why can't you shut up?

G.W. I like to talk.

RAFE I thought you came here tonight to be alone and not talk to anyone.

G.W. I did.

RAFE Then why the hell don't you do that?

G.W. I can't. You ruined the evening. Remember?

RAFE I don't need to be reminded of that.

G.W. So what do you do that you have to sit all day?

RAFE I don't feel like talking right now.

G.W. You wouldn't believe this, but I'd rather talk to my horses—well actually any animal for that matter. Don't like people much, for a species at the top of the alleged evolutionary ladder—well I'd rather talk to a horse.

RAFE You aren't ever gonna just sit there are you?

G.W. No.

RAFE You're just gonna keep rattling on and on.

G.W. I think a lot of people think the way I do, I mean why do so many people have pets then? Obviously people don't rate very high anymore. I was thinking of getting a dog.

RAFE Good for you.

G.W. Yeah. A basset-hound. I always thought they were neat dogs. I mean they're the Hush Puppies dog so how could you not like a basset-hound?

RAFE You're gonna get a basset-hound?

G.W. Thinkin' about it.

RAFE I had a basset-hound when I was a kid.

G.W. You did?

RAFE I did.

[RAFE *sits at the table*]

G.W. Isn't that something. Well it just goes to show you, great minds think alike.

RAFE Mr. Jiggs. I haven't thought about him in years. God he was a great dog. [*turns to* G.W.] When I was a kid we ...

G.W. Yeah?

RAFE Nothing.

G.W. So they're good dogs, basset-hounds?

RAFE They're great dogs. Mr. Jiggs was ... well that was a long time ago.

G.W. Oh.

[*pause*] Now we go to motorcade—

RAFE What?

G.W. Nothing.

[*pause*] So what do you do that you sit all day?

RAFE I work in an office.

G.W. Sounds boring.

RAFE I'm not in it enough to get bored.

G.W. So what do you do when you're not in the office?

RAFE I'm a seismologist for an oil company.

G.W. [*overlapping*] A wire man?

RAFE Yeah. A wire man.

G.W. You find oil by bouncing radio signals through the ground—sorta underground sonar.

RAFE That's a decent, half-assed, layman's explanation. Most people don't know what a seismologist does.

G.W. I read a lot. It's sorta this hobby I picked up. Isn't it something, I can pick your favourite song, and the dog I'm gonna buy is the same kind you had as a kid. I guess it's like Mr. Disney says, it's a small world after all.

RAFE Can we just sit now?

[*Pause*]

G.W. I wonder why Glen Campbell hasn't had a huge hit record in so long?

Murray Oliver (G.W.) and Ted Atherton (RAFE)
Photographer: Dina Almeida

RAFE [*exasperated*] I don't know.

G.W. He's been married god knows how many times, he's got a slew of kids, you'd think he'd need a hit all the time just to keep up with the alimony payments.

[*Pause.* G.W. *sings the first line of 'Galveston'*]

RAFE Don't sing.

G.W. Sorry, I got this thing for Glen Campbell. Broke my heart.

RAFE Glen Campbell broke your heart?

G.W. Not Glen Campbell. This guy I knew. He had this one Glen Campbell tape and we used to play it over and over. He, [*to* RAFE] he broke my heart. How about you Rafe, you ever have a broken heart?

RAFE No.

G.W. Everyone's had a broken heart, you have to, I think it's a rule. Not even once?

RAFE No. I don't think so. I was never very lucky that way.

G.W. I believe you make your own luck.

RAFE Good for you.

G.W. Never had a broken heart, hard to believe.

RAFE Believe what you want to.

G.W. I mean you're not bad looking, late twenties—

RAFE Try early thirties.

G.W. Really? you don't look a day over, say twenty-nine. Okay so you don't have much of a sense of humour ...

RAFE Will you shut up.

G.W. And you're rude.

RAFE And you never shut up.

G.W. You sure no one's ever broke your heart?

RAFE I'm sure.

G.W. That's sad.

RAFE That's my business.

G.W. I would've thought ...

RAFE What's with the twenty questions?

G.W. You seem a little uptight.

RAFE I am not uptight.

G.W. You don't seem very comfortable.

RAFE The bench's rock hard.

G.W. Being gay.

RAFE I hate that word.

G.W. It's just a word.

RAFE I don't like it.

G.W. It denotes a lifestyle.

RAFE I have a life. I don't have a lifestyle.

G.W. It has nothing to do with what you do in bed.

RAFE What I choose to do with my life is my business.

G.W. [*overlapping*] I agree with you one hundred percent.

RAFE I'm not like Danny.

G.W. You don't have to be.

RAFE I won't wear a sign.

G.W. No one said you have to.

RAFE Then why the hell don't you leave me alone.

G.W. Because, if you'll pardon the pun, you don't seem very happy.

RAFE I've got my reasons.

G.W. You're about the unhappiest person I've ever met.

RAFE So what if I am?

G.W. Can't be happy being unhappy.

RAFE Thank you doctor.

G.W. You don't seem very comfortable that's all.

RAFE That's my problem.

G.W. So what are the reasons?

RAFE Hey Kenny you can come and get me now ...

G.W. Why are you so miserable?

RAFE It's just the way it is.

G.W. It doesn't have to be, does it?

RAFE I don't want to talk about it.

G.W. You should—

RAFE [*overlapping*] I don't want to.

G.W. ... with someone.

RAFE Easier said than done.

G.W. How come?

RAFE I'm a private person.

G.W. Are you sayin' no one knows you're g—, no one knows?

RAFE It's not public knowledge.

G.W. No wonder you feel uncomfortable.

RAFE There's more to it than that. I suppose everyone knows about you.

G.W. My mom, who insists it's a phase, an awfully long phase but still a phase, my dad, who kicked me off the farm with words to the effect that I'm killing my mother *and* he won't be able to show his face in the beer parlour for 'hell knows how long.' My brother, who's cool. Friends. Jimmy. Cindy, my first girlfriend, well I guess you could say my last girlfriend, my only girlfriend actually, she knows. Actually we're pretty good friends.

RAFE You're lucky.

G.W. You make your own luck.

RAFE Then you're braver than I am.

G.W. It doesn't have anything to do with being brave. It's just knowing who and what you are. I'm a fag. That's what I am. Once I figured that out everything else fell into place. You don't have to wear a sign. I don't. I don't offer it up, but if someone asks, I tell them. One of the guys I work with, he knows.

RAFE I couldn't stand that. I couldn't take the stress.

G.W. He's pretty cool about it. He used to ask me, 'How come a young buck like you isn't keeping some young lady warm at night?' I used to tell him I couldn't find anyone I liked, which was sort of true. Then one day we were riding, checking the fences, we stopped for coffee an' he asked me.

RAFE [*incredulous*] An' you tole him?

G.W. He asked, I told him.

RAFE I just don't think it's anyone else's business.

G.W. You can't carry it around with you.

RAFE That's not really the problem.

G.W. You married?

RAFE Get real.

G.W. You wouldn't be the first.

RAFE I know.

G.W. Got a girlfriend?

RAFE No.

G.W. So what's stopping you.

RAFE If I was going to tell someone, which I'm not, even if
I thought it was the big problem that you seem to think it is
and I don't, I wouldn't know who to tell.

G.W. Start with your friends.

RAFE That's easier said than done.

G.W. [*overlapping*] If they're your friends they'll understand.

RAFE [*overlapping*] If I went berserk in a shopping mall dressed as
the Easter bunny, and murdered a dozen people while shouting
'The Ballad of the Green Berets' at the top of my lungs, my
friends would understand. This they wouldn't understand.

G.W. Straight friends.

RAFE They're not perfect but they are my friends.

G.W. Brothers, sisters.

RAFE Only child.

G.W. You don't have any … fag friends?

RAFE No.

G.W. You know Jimmy.

RAFE I don't 'know' Jimmy.

G.W. You're here.

RAFE I met him a long time ago, I run into him sometimes.
He nagged me to show up.

G.W. He's like that.

RAFE Jimmy's not the kind of person I'd have as a friend.

G.W. You're too old for him anyways.

RAFE I didn't mean that.

G.W. I know what you mean. Jimmy's a little flaky. I know he
invites me because he thinks something's going to happen.
It won't, but he keeps hoping.

RAFE I don't want to hear this.

G.W. You really don't know any other fags?

RAFE No.

G.W. Then what you need is more fag friends.

RAFE I don't think that's the answer.

G.W. You need to feel comfortable.

RAFE Whether or not anyone knows I'm a fag isn't the problem.

G.W. What about someone you meet cruising?

RAFE I don't think so.

G.W. You don't have a very good attitude.

RAFE Cruising's a big game. It's a joke. Nobody wants to get involved. They're looking for sex and once they find it, that's it. It's nothing but a game ...

G.W. That you play along with.

RAFE I don't make the rules.

G.W. And you don't do anything to change them.

RAFE I pick someone up the last thing I wanna do is talk to them. I can't wait to get it done and when it's done all I wanna do is get to hell away from them as soon as I can.

G.W. Just good, old-fashioned, anonymous sex.

RAFE It's just sex, no one wants to get involved.

G.W. No wonder you've never met anyone you liked.

RAFE I've met people, just not anyone I'd want for a friend. You don't make friends cruising, you find people to have sex with the next time you see them.

G.W. I met a guy I liked once, but that was a long time ago, years ago, actually.

RAFE There was this one guy ...

G.W. And you said it couldn't be done.

RAFE He was a nice guy, not the usual grab and grope. I remember we talked. Talked a lot. Before and after. Told me he wouldn't mind seeing me again. I thought that would be okay, you know. He gave me his number, told me to call him.

G.W. So'd you call him?

RAFE Yeah.

G.W. And you said it would be hard.

RAFE He lied. He gave me the number for time and temperature.

The time was nine-thirty. The temperature was fifteen degrees.

G.W. That's the way it goes sometimes.

RAFE That's the way it goes all the time. How about you? How do you meet someone?

G.W. I don't get out much, I mean I'm human like everyone else, but like I said I don't like people much, which is not to say I sit at home every night, just I don't go out much.

RAFE Oh.

G.W. Okay. So start at the beginning. Your parents. Nothing says yours have to be like mine.

RAFE I can't.

G.W. Sure you can.

RAFE I can't.

G.W. I know what you're thinking, it's hard, it'll kill 'em, well it didn't kill mine. Believe me. Your mom was probably someone who took an interest in you, helped you with your homework, made sure you joined the Cub Scouts, was always there to talk to if you needed to talk. Made you feel like you were the most important person in the world. Am I right?

RAFE Yeah.

G.W. Mine wasn't. My mom didn't care about what I did as long as I didn't make her look bad. She's always been more worried about appearances and her reputation.

RAFE Maybe she just wanted the best for you.

G.W. She wanted the perfect son, she didn't get it. I'm sorry. I really am sometimes. You love your mom, you're lucky.

RAFE You don't?

G.W. I like her but I don't love her. It's always been like that since I was a little kid. Too bad you can't choose your parents.

RAFE I'm sorry you feel like that.

G.W. So you mean you've never met anyone you ever liked, ever wanted to see again? I mean aside from the time and temperature guy?

RAFE No. [*he starts pacing*]

G.W. You've never been out driving, seen someone ...

RAFE No.

G.W. ... stopped to talk to them ...

RAFE No.

G.W. ... found yourself attracted to them ...

RAFE No.

G.W. ... go for coffee with them ...

RAFE No.

G.W. ... maybe sit in a Country Style Donuts ...

RAFE No. No. No. No. No. No.

G.W. [*overlapping*] ... talk and yak, get to know them ...

RAFE No.

G.W. Not ever?

RAFE Not ever.

G.W. That's sad Rafe.

RAFE Thanks for pointing that out to me.

G.W. You're sure, not even once?

RAFE [*overlapping*] *Yes*, I'm sure. Are you happy now? There is no one, there's never been anyone, and there probably won't ever be anyone.

G.W. Rafe, I'm sorry.

[RAFE *does not respond*]

I mean I didn't mean to bring you down.

[RAFE *does not respond*]

Rafe, you okay? Hey c'mon man, it's gonna be okay, don't sweat it, we'll work it out, I mean you're not the first person who's ever felt alone, you won't be the last ...

RAFE I'll do just fine, you don't have to worry about me.

G.W. [*crossing to* RAFE] I know, it's just ... Don't get yourself so worked up, I mean c'mon ... C'mon, just take it easy.

[G.W. *puts his hand on* RAFE*'s left shoulder*]

RAFE [*trying to shake him off*] Don't touch me.
G.W. Rafe, it's okay.

[G.W. *places his right hand on* RAFE*'s shoulder and begins to massage his shoulders.* RAFE *pushes him away*]

RAFE Fuck you ya bastard. I don't believe this I really don't.
G.W. Believe what?
RAFE I don't need your understanding.
G.W. [*overlapping*] What's the matter?
RAFE I should have known better.
G.W. Rafe—
RAFE You can knock it off 'cause I know what you're up to.
G.W. I'm not up to anything.
RAFE [*overlapping*] Don't try an' bullshit me.
G.W. [*overlapping*] I'm not.
RAFE I can see it all, if you'll excuse the pun, laid out in front of me, so don't bother.
G.W. All I've 'bothered' to do is try and make you feel better about Danny.
RAFE This isn't about Danny.
G.W. Yeah, you're right, okay so I tried to make you feel better.
RAFE Why didn't you just mind your own bloody business?
G.W. Because you're feeling bad, nobody should feel that bad.
RAFE Sticking your nose in where it don't belong ...
G.W. [*overlapping*] That's your opinion.
RAFE ... so you could play the sensitive faggot.
G.W. Fine. You wanna be miserable then be miserable 'cause it's damned clear to me that you got no one to blame but yourself. You're a loud, foul-mouthed, cold-blooded son-of-a-bitch with no sense of humour or life. You want me to shut up and mind my own business? Fine. You do the same and we'll both be happy.

249

[G.W. *crosses to the table, sits down, stares, not looking at* RAFE. *Long pause*]

    Do not lament, do not cry.

RAFE What?

G.W. Thought you were gonna sit there and be quiet?

RAFE Thought you might wanna talk.

G.W. I don't feel like talking

RAFE I do.

G.W. Good for you.

[*Pause.* G.W. *turns his cap around, puts it on the right way*]

RAFE So you're a Tigers fan?

G.W. No I'm not.

RAFE Then what's with the hat?

G.W. I'm a Magnum fan.

RAFE A what?

G.W. Tom Selleck. Magnum P.I., on TV, he wore a Tigers hat.
    I'm a Tom Selleck fan.

RAFE Guess somebody has to be.

[G.W. *looks at* RAFE. *Pause*]

    So … you raise horses.

G.W. You aren't gonna just sit there and be quiet, are you?

RAFE So you raise horses.

G.W. Yeah.

RAFE Must be fun.

G.W. It's hard work.

RAFE Yeah guess it is. About what I said.

G.W. You don't have to explain it to me.

RAFE I know what you were trying to do and I appreciate it,
    I do. Just, I've never had anyone bother before an' 'cause
    I didn't … I mean this sounds real stupid but I thought …

oh shit ... I thought you were trying to get on my good side ...

G.W. Do you have a good side?

RAFE I shouldn't have gotten mad okay? You're right. I shouldn't have said the things that I said. I need more fag friends, I don't have anyone I can talk to. Just, I guess you're probably right, I should feel better about myself, maybe I'd be more comfortable, maybe I wouldn't let guys like Danny get to me, it's just I don't think it's gonna change things.

G.W. Don't know unless you try.

RAFE In Saskatoon, I cruise Spadina, or Scarth when I'm in Regina. I look at everyone walking around, no one talks to anyone, the cars go 'round and 'round and no one stops. You walk past someone and your eyes meet, you look each other right in the eye, but you don't stop, you don't talk. Everyone's there for the same reason, all the lonely people looking for the same thing. I walk for hours, up and down the same strip of sidewalk, hours, and no one says a word to me, and I keep walking, hoping a car will stop, or someone'll ask the time just to start a conversation, but they never do. And by then I don't give a damn about getting it on, I just want someone to talk to me, to let me know I'm there, that I exist. That's all it is deep down inside, having someone to talk to. Companionship. Having someone there, even if it's just for a while. I watch all the old men in big cars cruising the block leering at all the blond, blue-eyed, eighteen-year-old hustlers in their tight-ass jeans and I wonder, am I gonna end up like that? All alone. Another old man who's so desperate to feel a part of the world, to feel alive and not so alone, he'll shell out thirty bucks to have some kid blow him.

G.W. It doesn't have to be like that.

RAFE People get lonely. Sometimes you don't want to be alone.

G.W. If I ever got to that point I'd blow my brains out. I wouldn't degrade myself like that. I've got pride in who I am.

Besides, I'm not going to get old.

RAFE Everyone gets old.

G.W. Maybe, but I'm not going to waste my time thinking about it.

RAFE All I know is I don't want to be alone anymore.

G.W. You don't know you will be.

RAFE I've been having this nightmare. I've got AIDS, and, and I'm lying in this hospital bed but I'm looking down at myself from a corner of the room. I'm alone. Day after day, no one ever comes to visit. Ever.

G.W. If you're worried, take a test.

RAFE I did.

G.W. And?

RAFE It was negative.

G.W. Then you've got nothing to worry about.

RAFE You been tested?

G.W. Do I look worried?

RAFE No. Why then all of a sudden am I having this nightmare?

G.W. You're afraid you'll die alone. You don't have anyone in your life, you're afraid you'll leave nothing behind. No one will remember you.

RAFE I'm scared.

G.W. But you can't let it rule your life.

RAFE Have you been to the dentist lately, you'd think they were dealing with radioactive waste, I'm surprised they don't come in wearing lead suits. And you're telling me I should feel better about myself.

G.W. Fuck you. If you're so worried avoid the risk. Live in a cave or become a monk. That's the way it is. What the hell is the big deal? The greatest mystery of life is when am I gonna die? People give themselves strokes worrying about it. You get the plague. You know the answer. No more mystery. No more worries. No more questions.

RAFE That's depressing.

G.W. That's realistic. In John Wayne's last movie, *The Shootist*, Jimmy Stewart tells him, [*does a Jimmy Stewart impression*] 'You have a cancer.' So he sets up his last gunfight so he'll die on his birthday. Has the headstone made up in advance.

RAFE That's morbid.

G.W. It's all in how you look at it.

RAFE I guess. 'Bout what I said.

G.W. Enough already.

RAFE I thought you were only talking to me to get me feeling bad so you could cheer me up, make me feel better an' then, well you know …

G.W. Know what.

RAFE I thought something would happen.

G.W. Oh yeah, like what?

RAFE I thought you were trying to pick me up.

G.W. And my mother thinks I've got problems.

RAFE I don't think that now. You were only trying to help. I know that now but I thought it was just gonna end up like all the other times.

G.W. I'd give you the number for time and temperature.

RAFE I thought if it was all a game …

G.W. Why put yourself through it. Well I'll tell you this, if I was trying to pick you up, you'd know it.

[G.W. *smiles at* RAFE, *then hands him his empty beer bottle*]

I need a beer.

[G.W. *exits.* RAFE *shakes his head, looks towards the house, smiles.* RAFE *walks around the table.* G.W. *enters*]

Well things seem to have returned to normal. Whatever that is.

RAFE What?

G.W. Inside. Things seem to have calmed down. They're downstairs playing video games. You could leave now, I don't think there'd be a problem.

RAFE Oh. You know you were asking earlier why I came here tonight. I'll tell you if you're still interested.

G.W. I thought you wanted to go.

RAFE Yeah I did.

G.W. You seemed in a big hurry before.

RAFE That was before.

G.W. Do whatever you want to.

RAFE You were asking why I came here tonight, well it might sound stupid but, I thought ... I thought I might meet someone.

G.W. That doesn't sound stupid.

RAFE Bet it's a night Danny won't soon forget.

G.W. Lighten up. We've been through this.

RAFE You're right. I did meet someone. I don't even know your name.

G.W. You can call me G.W.

RAFE G.W., eh. G.W., I'm Rafe. But you already know that. Thanks.

G.W. For what?

RAFE For listening to me.

G.W. That's me, always in the right place at the right time ...

RAFE You said I should have more fag friends. So how about it? Friends?

G.W. Just because I talked to you.

RAFE And listened. I mean it's not easy for me to talk, but it was easier, it's easy to be honest when you believe that someone really cares and it isn't a game, that they're listening and just not lying to you.

G.W. I guess it is.

RAFE Yeah.

G.W. So I'll be honest with you, you like honesty so much. I lied.

RAFE What?

G.W. I lied to you.

254

RAFE You're kidding, right?

G.W. I'm very serious.

RAFE I don't believe you.

G.W. Believe me. I thought you wanted to get out of here.

RAFE I did.

G.W. Then why didn't you?

RAFE Everyone was pissed off at me 'cause I punched Danny, he landed on the coffee table ...

G.W. Danny's fine.

RAFE What?

G.W. He's fine. Not a scratch on him.

RAFE He landed on the coffee table. You said there was blood and glass everywhere.

G.W. No blood, lotsa glass.

RAFE You said ...

G.W. After you hit Danny and took off out here, Danny turned to go after you, someone grabbed his arm, he spun around and knocked a twenty-four out of Kenny's arms. It landed on the coffee table.

RAFE So Danny's not cut up? Kenny doesn't want to beat the crap out of me?

G.W. He was more worried about the beer than he was about Danny.

RAFE You said, you told me they were gonna beat the crap out of me, they were inside waiting for me ...

G.W. I told you, I lied.

RAFE Then they weren't waiting for me?

G.W. No. Actually Kenny passed out, and they moved the party to the rec room.

RAFE Then you lied about everything.

G.W. Yes.

RAFE Why?

G.W. You can go.

255

RAFE Fuck you. I wanna know what the fuck is going on. Why did you lie?

G.W. Like I said I wanted to see how you've been, how you were.

RAFE Do I believe that?

G.W. Believe whatever you want to believe.

RAFE You've lost me.

G.W. Wouldn't be the first time. Drink your beer. Oh that's right you don't drink. Anymore. You don't have to stay here.

RAFE What the fuck is going on?

G.W. You still here?

RAFE What the fuck is going on here?

G.W. I told you.

RAFE I wanna know why you lied.

G.W. It just happened.

RAFE It just happened?

G.W. If it makes you feel any better I didn't mean to.

RAFE You said you wanted to see how I've been.

G.W. Grammatical error. I used the wrong tense, excuse me.

RAFE And what's this, 'You don't drink. *Anymore.*'

G.W. Look, I've told you, you don't have to stay here, you can go.

RAFE I'm not going anywhere until you tell me why you did this.

G.W. And if I don't tell you what are you gonna do, punch me out?

RAFE I believed you because you listened, you make me feel better, then you tell me this. You think it was easy for me to tell you what I did?

G.W. No I don't. But you did tell me.

RAFE Because you kept me here, and I wanna know why.

G.W. [*overlapping*] I told you.

RAFE [*overlapping*] I thought we could be friends.

G.W. [*overlapping*] You don't have to stay here you can go.

RAFE [*overlapping*] Then you tell me you lied to me.

G.W. [*overlapping*] Forget it Rafe, just forget it.

RAFE [*overlapping*] I don't wanna forget it, I wanna know why.

G.W. [*overlapping*] It just happened.

RAFE [*overlapping*] Is this your kick?

G.W. [*overlapping*] Why don't you just leave?

RAFE [*overlapping*] Is this your thing, is it?

G.W. [*overlapping*] Rafe, fuck off okay?

RAFE [*overlapping*] You get off on this, don't you?

G.W. [*overlapping*] Rafe—

RAFE [*overlapping*] I thought you were different.

G.W. [*overlapping*] Rafe—

RAFE [*overlapping*] You're no different than anyone else.

G.W. Raphael.

[*Beat*]

RAFE How do you know my name?

[G.W. *does not respond*]

I don't tell anyone that. How do you know that?

G.W. You don't remember me do you?

[RAFE *does not respond*]

Ask a stupid question.

RAFE We've met?

G.W. We've met.

RAFE I don't remember.

G.W. That's obvious.

RAFE When?

G.W. It was a Saturday night, the August long weekend. I was nineteen, I'll be twenty-six in October, six years ago.

RAFE Tonight.

G.W. Really?

RAFE It's the August long weekend.

G.W. I never realized.

RAFE You were nineteen, I was twenty-five.

G.W. You were driving a Chevy half-ton.

RAFE I always drive a Chevy.

G.W. License plate CSW 265.

RAFE An '82 Silverado. [*pause*] I was drinking then.

G.W. I know.

RAFE It's not that I don't believe you.

G.W. If you'd left when I told you to …

RAFE But I didn't. I swear to you, G.W., I don't remember you. If you want the truth I don't remember a whole lot.

G.W. [*overlapping*] That's understandable.

RAFE I been dry two years now and I still run into people who seem to know me but I … I don't have a clue who they are, or how we met, or why. Sometimes something just pops into my head, a name, a song, something or someone looks familiar, and I don't know why. I don't remember meeting you. There's a year and a half, two years of my life I can't remember. [*pause*] So how did we meet?

G.W. Rafe, we don't have to go through this.

RAFE I do.

G.W. I was sitting on the grass on Spadina past the park, near the Broadway Bridge, there was this '52 T-Bird. I was looking at the car and the next thing I know there you were. We started talking.

RAFE And then?

G.W. You asked me what I was doing. I told you I'd just hit town, told you about the old man and you said, 'Let's go for coffee.'

RAFE And things went the way they usually do.

G.W. No. Not at all.

RAFE Oh?

G.W. We went for coffee and we talked. Sat in a Country Style Donuts talking 'til about four in the morning, went for a drive, drove all over town, went back to the Country Style, had a bite to eat, talked, then we drove around and talked some more.

RAFE What the hell did we have to talk about?

G.W. Everything. Books, music, politics, you name it. Sports, crops, weather, being fags, everything. We just talked, and then about seven in the morning you offered me the use of your couch.

RAFE I didn't ask you to ...

G.W. No. You said sex wasn't everything. That, for some reason, impressed the hell out of me.

RAFE Did we ever—

G.W. That's not important.

RAFE I'd like to know.

G.W. We did, and if you need to know, it was great.

RAFE I didn't need to know that. Then what?

G.W. I hung around for a couple of days. You said I could stay if I wanted but I wanted to see some friends who were living in town. You said I was welcome any time. I came by a couple of times after that, but you were never home.

RAFE I was real busy, work was nuts. I wasn't home much.

G.W. So I stayed with Cindy, my only girlfriend. Found a job. I stopped by from time to time but you weren't home, and then I went by once and you'd moved.

RAFE I was working out of Regina for a while, then Calgary, I was moving around a lot.

G.W. I didn't know how to get in touch with you.

RAFE Why did you want to?

G.W. You were fun to be with. You could talk a blue streak but you listened. I was bust-up about the old man kicking me out and you listened. You were a friend when I didn't have any friends.

RAFE It was the booze.

G.W. It was who you were.

RAFE I was different then.

G.W. You're the same person, you just don't have that spark you used to have.

RAFE It was the booze. I was ... I am an alcoholic. I was uninhibited when I was loaded, and I was rather uninhibited for years.

G.W. So what happened?

RAFE I wish I could tell you what one thing it was, if it was just one thing. I woke up one morning and it wasn't worth it any more. I didn't know where the hell I was, who the person next to me was or how I got there. I got tired, tired of the one-night stands. Whatever thrill there once was in riding all night, hoping, searching, just vanished. I was drinking too much. I'd go to bed drunk, wake up half-drunk, be drunk by lunch. I almost killed a guy driving home one night. My parents died. Two years ago. A drunk. Crossed over the centre line. Hit 'em head on. And all this time ... I don't know what happened, I just know it did.

G.W. I'm sorry about your folks.

RAFE Thanks. So ... what was tonight all about then?

G.W. I wanted to see you and talk to you.

RAFE I don't recognize you.

G.W. I knew it was you the minute I saw you.

RAFE Why'd you lie?

G.W. I wanted to talk to you, to see how you'd been, I mean I just couldn't say hi and then 'bye, I had to keep you here, so I made up the story about Danny and then you were so upset about it, I had to lie to support the first lie and before I knew it ...

RAFE You'd backed yourself into a corner.

G.W. I went in for a beer, I knew it was time for you to go and I came out and told you you could leave but you didn't. Then you started in with how honest I was and I felt like a shit, I felt bad about lying so then I had to tell you.

RAFE That doesn't tell me why you did it.

G.W. I wanted to talk to you.

RAFE That's an excuse, not a reason.

G.W. I wanted to talk to you.

RAFE So you lie, you manipulate the situation, you manipulate me? That's a helluva lot of trouble to talk to someone who doesn't remember you.

G.W. I think you do.

RAFE You hope I do.

G.W. Yes I do.

RAFE What's G.W. stand for?

G.W. You know.

RAFE I don't know what I know.

G.W. Your mom's name is ... was Flo. Your last name's Joseph. Your middle name is Michael. You used to have a picture of Mr. Jiggs near the phone.

RAFE Okay, I believe you.

G.W. You remember, I know you do.

RAFE I wish I did.

G.W. You said you'd never forget me.

RAFE I might have said a lot of things.

G.W. The guy with the Glen Campbell tape, that was you.

RAFE I never owned a Glen Campbell tape.

G.W. It was a tape of mixed music. 'Lineman' was one of them.

RAFE I don't know what to say.

G.W. You don't have to say anything.

RAFE I don't know what I can say.

G.W. You said my name was funny. Sounded like some town in Australia.

RAFE That helps a lot. I guess.

G.W. There was something else.

RAFE Probably.

G.W. Verses.

RAFE Verses.

G.W. Verses. 'Now we go to motorcade / pride of pookas on

parade / If I wake before I die / pooka pooka pooka pie.'

RAFE I taught you that?

G.W. You gave me the book. *The Ink Truck* by William Kennedy. You said if I didn't get any understanding of politics or social- ism at least there was this silly little verse.

RAFE Okay.

G.W. And, 'Do not lament, do not cry / live your life the way you must ...

RAFE ... a brave heart does not deny.' [*pause*] Why am I here?

G.W. I told you

RAFE That's not good enough. You could have talked to me, we could have gotten along fine, but you kept me here. You didn't have to tell me you lied, you could have made something up on the spot, you're awfully good at that, so why didn't you? Talking to me isn't a good enough reason.

G.W. It's good enough for me.

RAFE For fuck's sake cut the bullshit Griffin! ... Griffin?

G.W. That's my name don't wear it out.

RAFE Griffin. [*pause*] Griffin ... Welles, like Alice Springs. Is this why you kept me here? So I'd come to remember you if I was forced to.

G.W. I wanted to talk to you ...

RAFE [*overlapping*] I don't understand. I remember your name, bits and pieces, but there's no face, it might not be you.

G.W. I wanted to talk to you. Because you saved my life. [*beat*] I was sittin' lookin at the T-Bird, wondering where the hell I was gonna spend the night, all these old men kept offering me money to sleep with them, then you showed up.

RAFE I'm sure my motives weren't totally honourable.

G.W. You saved my life. I was feelin' lost. I was alone. I was scared an' you come along, we go for coffee and we're drivin' and we're talking about the weather, but we're talking about how clouds form, not if it'll rain but why it rains. I'd never read more than three books in my entire life and you're talking about Shakespeare, the economy, sex, politics ... All I'd ever listened to was heavy metal and the next thing I know I'm listening to everything from Mozart, Glen Campbell, the Grateful Dead and show tunes. I left the farm thinking I was nothing, that I was sick, that I didn't fit into the world and that the world had no place for me. I wasn't scared after I met you. I figured out for myself that I did fit. But I couldn't have if I hadn't met you. You can go now, you don't have to stay.

[*Pause*]

RAFE [*remembering*] You sip your tea off the spoon to see if it's got enough sugar.

G.W. I told you, you don't have to stay.

RAFE Your cloud's moving.

G.W. Nothing remains the same. This was supposed to be so simple. Why are you staying around?

RAFE You don't want me to?

G.W. No Rafe I don't.

RAFE Just, I thought, tonight I thought I made a friend. A new friend, a new, old friend.

G.W. Don't be so nice to me.

RAFE You want me to punch you in the face?

G.W. I don't want to be your friend.

RAFE Then why did you go through all this?

G.W. I wasn't supposed to get to know you again, we were gonna talk. You used to talk so freely but you ... Tonight you're this, angry, cynical tough-guy, and I had to know what happened, but it gets harder. You're telling me how you're feeling, and I can't stop myself caring about you, and even when you turned mean I thought there was still a way out, and I keep trying to understand everything you're telling me, and I know I'm getting in deeper 'cause all I can see is me sitting there the

263

night we met, you helping me like you did. Then you start telling me I'm honest ... you know the rest. I can't be your friend Rafe.

RAFE I'm not talking about sleeping together.

G.W. We can't be friends. We can't be anything.

RAFE You didn't go through all this to tell me that.

G.W. It's not happening again, I won't let it.

RAFE You're not making any sense.

G.W. I fell for you ya dumb fuck. I was crazy about you. And maybe I still am. You think if I'm your friend I'm gonna change everything you've talked about tonight? You think you won't be lonely, that I can make everything better, or you'll under-stand the world or yourself any better? I can't do that for you.

RAFE I'm not the same person who punched Danny in the mouth.

G.W. In the long run you'll be just as miserable, maybe more. I'm not going to be responsible for that.

RAFE That makes me feel real good.

G.W. Don't take everything so personally.

RAFE How am I supposed to take it then?

G.W. Just go, Rafe.

RAFE We can't even be friends?

G.W. Rafe dammit, I've said all I'm going to say.

RAFE You haven't said anything.

G.W. Rafe, turn around and walk away and give me credit for knowing the right thing to do. Trust me.

RAFE Tell me why.

G.W. I won't.

RAFE Then I'll sit here 'til you do.

G.W. Then you're gonna sit there for a helluva long time.

RAFE Griffin ...

G.W. I'm not gonna say it.

RAFE You're hiding something.

G.W. I'm not hiding anything. It's all there in front of you.

RAFE Then you're lying.

G.W. I'm not lying. I don't lie all the time.

RAFE Only to get what you want.

G.W. I'm not gonna say it, I'm not.

RAFE You said it's all there in front of me. What's in front of me?

G.W. It's everything we've talked about.

RAFE Everything we talked about. Great, a place to start, should I feel grateful?

G.W. Feel any fucking thing you want to.

RAFE You're starting to swear a lot.

G.W. I'm a subject of my environment.

RAFE Okay, so what did we talk about? Or, what did I talk about? I talked about how I felt, people lying to each other,

[G.W. *looks at him*]

being alone, no one wants to get involved, no one talks to you when they're cruising, my nightmare. You talked about Glen Campbell, your folks, leaving the farm, why more people don't like country music, Glen Campbell breaking your heart, and the John Wayne movie you liked so much.

G.W. [*overlapping*] I never said I liked it.

RAFE Okay so it's not your favourite. Then there was why you lied, why you kept me here, how we met, what I don't remember, your name. That, Griffin, is the gist of it.

G.W. Except what you forgot.

RAFE What did I forget?

G.W. I told you I'm not going to say it.

RAFE Okay, so I forgot something. [*beat*] There's who knows you're a fag, that's not what's important, anonymous sex, sensitive faggot—well you know how that went—more of my whining, parents, you can't choose your parents. That's it.

G.W. Not quite.

RAFE I'm gettin' old, I forget easy, excuse me.

G.W. And I'll be twenty-six in October.

RAFE And I'll be thirty-two in January, we're getting older, so what?

G.W. So I have to piss.

RAFE What did I forget?

[**G.W.** *exits.* **RAFE** *stands. He thinks aloud, repeating bits and pieces of what he has remembered about what they discussed*]

People lying to each other, his folks, leaving the farm, Glen Campbell breaking your heart, the John Wayne movie you liked so much, I never said I liked it, I don't fit in, I feel alone, I'll be twenty-six in October ... What else? My nightmare, the greatest mystery in life, the John Wayne movie, everyone gets old, not me. [*he looks towards the house as he realizes*] Oh fuck.

[**G.W.** *enters*]

G.W. You're persistent. Penny for your thoughts.

RAFE Don't make jokes.

G.W. Figured it out then did you?

RAFE Yeah. Awfully nice of you to let me do that.

G.W. I told you to leave.

RAFE But I stayed.

G.W. Rafe, you wanna be friends, you wanna call me up and say let's go to a movie or go fishing, and that's fine, but what are you gonna do when you phone and there's no answer.

RAFE Call back.

G.W. And when the phone's disconnected? What then? After the movies and the fishing trips, all the anythings that might add up to somethings.

RAFE I should decide that, not you.

G.W. You're afraid of ending up alone, you're scared of that.

RAFE You're just gonna give up? What about your parents? Your friends? What about your horses?

G.W. My parents will know when they have to know. I'm not telling anyone else and I don't expect you to.

RAFE You think I would?

G.W. The horses will be okay, I gave my notice and they'll be well cared for and looked after.

RAFE Then what?

G.W. I was thinking I'd go to B.C. Always wanted to see the mountains and the ocean, they say if you come from the Prairies you have an affinity with the ocean, the way a field ripples in the breeze, it's like the waves of the ocean.

RAFE You're gonna run away.

G.W. I'm gonna do what I want, what I feel is right.

RAFE And if I want ...

G.W. It doesn't include you. You're alone, you want someone, you want someone that wants you as much as you want them, you see red sails in the sunset and everything that goes with it. It won't be with me. I'm not gonna give you something that's gonna tear you apart. I won't give you something and then rip it away from you. I wish I could.

RAFE You don't give me much credit.

G.W. I know you. I knew you then and I know you now. Yeah, things have happened but you're still a kind man Rafe, a giving, generous man. When your head's not messed up, and I'm not gonna hurt you.

RAFE I wish I hadn't figured it out.

G.W. It wouldn't change anything.

[*Pause*]

RAFE Are you sure? Are you absolutely sure?

G.W. I'm sure. I've been in the hospital once already. *Rafe,* I'm gonna die. There I said it. I said I wasn't going to but I did. I'm gonna die. And I'm not ending up in some hospital with a bunch of tubes sticking out of me, wasting away.

267

RAFE You'll be alone.

G.W. I'm my own best company. That's fine with me.

RAFE It's not fine. It's not, no one should be alone, if it were me …

G.W. It's not you.

RAFE It could be.

G.W. Rafe, this isn't the fucking flu. It's more than getting thin and losing my hair, I'm gonna have tumours the size of grape-fruits all over my body.

[RAFE *looks at* G.W., *who looks away. He looks at the house, then back to* G.W. *Looks up at the sky*]

RAFE The cloud, it's formed into a thunderhead. Maybe it'll rain after all.

G.W. Just leave me alone, please.

RAFE No.

G.W. Then why do you wanna stay? I don't need pity. Besides, you're scared, that's what you said, you're scared you'll get the plague. You wanna be friends. Why do you wanna do this? Be friends for a couple of months then I die. We can't be friends. I don't want you hanging around, gettin' involved, and I don't need it—falling in love with you again. No way. What kind of friendship is that?

RAFE Better than the one we had, the one I can't remember.

[RAFE *crosses. He comes up behind* G.W. *and places his hand on his shoulder.* G.W. *turns and pushes* RAFE *away.* RAFE *grabs ahold of his arm. When* RAFE *wraps his arms around* G.W., *he tries to push* RAFE *away.* RAFE *locks his fingers together and holds on as* G.W. *tries to break* RAFE*'s hold*]

G.W. Don't. Don't touch me. I don't need you and I don't want you touching me. Let go of me. Leave me alone.

[**G.W.** *thrashes, trying to shake* **RAFE** *off. Slowly* **G.W.** *stops trying, gives in, and buries his head in* **RAFE**'s *shoulder.* **RAFE** *relaxes his grip and slides his arms around* **G.W.** *and hugs him.* **G.W.** *breaks away. There is an extremely loud crack of thunder*]

   [*looks at the sky*] It's not gonna rain, it's all noise an' no action. [*he turns to* **RAFE**] You don't wanna do this.

RAFE You have this bad habit of always telling me what to do.

G.W. You have to think about yourself.

RAFE I am. I am.

[**G.W.** *looks at* **RAFE** *and falls into his arms.* **RAFE** *wraps his arms around* **G.W.** *There is another loud crack of thunder. Lights fade slowly to black*]

[*End*]

Flesh and Blood

by Colin Thomas

Flesh and Blood was first produced by Theatre Direct Canada and premiered at 26 Berkeley Street, the Stage Downstairs, in Toronto in April 1991 with the following cast:

JIM, Mark Saunders
ALLAN, David Orth
RALPH, Rob Osborne
SHERRI-LEE, Amanda Stepto

Director: JoAnn McIntyre
Set and Lighting Designer: Graeme Thomson
Costume Designer: Stephanie Tjelios
Stage Manager: Tony Ambrosi
Production Manager: Simon Clemo
Scenic Painter: David Rayfield
Sound Designer: Evan Turner
Artistic Director: Andrey Tarasiuk

Flesh and Blood was originally commissioned by Green Thumb Theatre for Young People.

For permission to perform the play please contact:

Colin Thomas
2137 West First Avenue, Suite 43
Vancouver, Canada
V6K 1E7

Notes:

It may be helpful for designers to know that in the original production Graeme Thomson's set included two major playing areas. The first of these, JIM's apartment, consisted of a large living/dining room with two doorways leading off, one to the bedroom and bathroom, the other to the kitchen. The other major playing area was what director JoAnn McIntyre referred to as ALLAN's 'rage ramp.' This was an abstract set piece where the scene 'Hospital' was played. The rage ramp was also where ALLAN played the transitional sequences in which he smokes dope, drinks, and vents his fury. Those transitions evolved from JoAnn's vision and are now included in this script.

Anybody who's considering producing *Flesh and Blood* should know that, to the extent that it does work, this play works because of its honesty. The rough language and sexual explicitness are an essential part of that candidness and should be regarded as an asset rather than a liability.

Regarding ages: ALLAN is seventeen, JIM is about twenty-six.

One final, picky note: in the script, I refer to man called Luis. This is a Spanish name. It's important to get it right.

For Stuart

Flesh and Blood

Scenes

Looney Tunes

ALLAN's *room at the psychiatric clinic. Probably indicated with just a couple of chairs.* ALLAN's *right hand is bandaged*

JIM Nice place.

ALLAN For a loony bin.

JIM Yeah, well it's a lot better than Riverview. I visited a friend out there once. They got bars on the windows for Christ's sake.

[*Beat*]

I mean this place is more like a hotel. Nice rug. Half-decent colour scheme.

[*Beat*]

Looks like they treat you like a human being.

ALLAN Pretty funny clientele. If it's a hotel. I mean, if it's a hotel, I think they should check their guest list. You should see some of the tunes around here.

JIM Yeah. Pretty spooky, eh? This guy I saw on the way in, he was acting like the Hunchback of Notre Dame. You know the one I mean?

ALLAN Yeah, he's called Gregory.

JIM He doesn't even look like he's crazy. He looks like he's *acting* crazy. Maybe he's one of the staff. Under cover.

ALLAN I wouldn't know. I haven't been here that long.

JIM How long before I can get you out?

ALLAN Couple days. Somethin' like that. They said they want

277

me here for observation.

JIM How's it goin'?

[ALLAN *shrugs*]

How's your hand?

ALLAN Okay.

JIM You don't have to tell me anything if you don't want.

ALLAN It was Mom. Of course. You talk to her yet?

JIM [*shakes his head*] No. I thought I'd wait till I got it from you.

ALLAN [*nods*] It was nothing. It was just so stupid. I'm really in the wrong place here.

JIM Yeah. I know.

ALLAN She was cleaning out my room, which I didn't ask her to do in the first place. You know how she does that? And she must have been going through my garbage, like she was looking for something, like she's looking for some kind of clue that I was going to hell. And ... [*he starts to chuckle*]

JIM And what?

ALLAN She found it!

JIM What?

ALLAN A safe.

JIM You mean, like, a condom?

ALLAN A used one. Really nice.

JIM Oh, Christ.

ALLAN I mean me and Sherri-Lee got tired of freezing our asses off in the car. So we did it in my room a couple of times when she was out. I never thought she'd go through my garbage.

[JIM *nods*]

Can't you just see the look on her face?

JIM So then what? She attacked you with the kitchen knife?

ALLAN No. She waited till I got home. She must've been sitting up all night. [*chuckles*]

She was wearing a rubber glove. You know like the ones she uses to do the dishes? And she was waving this thing around between her little rubber fingers and going, 'How could you do this to me? How could you do this to me?' I felt like saying, 'I didn't do it to you, I did it to my girlfriend.' But then she starts crying. [*sighs*]

And so, like a complete asshole, I try to talk to her, like, to calm her down, but as soon as I do this, she turns into this absolute—bitch. And she starts quotin' the Bible at me and starts sayin' how she wished I'd never been born and how she wished she'd had an abortion an' that.

JIM Wait a minute. She actually said that?

ALLAN Yeah. Yeah, and I believe her, too. You wanna know exactly what she said? She said—let me get the words right now. She said, 'If I had lived in any other province than Saskatchewan, I would've had an abortion, because in those days I turned to the doctors and not to the Lord. So just think about that. Next time.'

JIM What the hell's that supposed to mean?

ALLAN Fucked if I know.

JIM You didn't hit her, did you?

ALLAN No. Whaddyou think I am? But I was pretty drunk already. So I just went out to the car, in the garage, and drank some more.

I dunno, it's like she's been even worse since you left. She's just always on my back about school an' that. Sometimes I'd just like to deck her, just to shut her up, but ...

JIM I know.

ALLAN It's like she's so crazy, she'd break into a million pieces.

JIM I know. I know.

[*Beat*]

ALLAN So I don't know why I did it. I can't even remember what I was thinking, but I just put my hand right through the garage window. Like my fist. It didn't even hurt. It was weird, like I was in a movie or somethin'. It's like I'm just standin' there, goin', 'Oh. Wow. I'm bleeding.' But then I go into the hospital—I mean the house—and Mom freaks out.

JIM So why'd they send you here?

ALLAN They thought I was trying to commit suicide. No way! No way.

[*quietly*] And my worker said I was violent.

JIM What'd you do?

ALLAN Nothing.

JIM What'd you do?

ALLAN Nothing. I told you. I stuck my hand through a window.

JIM Al, you can't ...

ALLAN [*interrupting*] And I told them—like when they first brought me in—I told them, no matter what, I didn't want to go back home. With her.

[*Pause*]

JIM You can come stay with me, if you want.

As soon as you get outta here. I don't have a helluva lotta room ...

ALLAN But what about your roommate, Ralph, an' that?

JIM That's okay. Ralph and I aren't roommates any more. You can stay as long as you want, but you'll probably want to go back in the fall. For school? I dunno. We'll work it out.

Just one thing, though. No drinking, 'kay? It just freaks me out. Your hand's bad enough. Okay?

ALLAN Okay.

JIM I mean it.

ALLAN Yeah, yeah. One drink an' I'm out. How 'bout that?

JIM We'll keep ya busy, eh?

So you think they'll trust me here? Like to let you come stay with me?

ALLAN Who cares what they say about it? What do they need to know? I told this one doctor I had a brother, but I left out all the good bits.

JIM [*laughs*] Good idea. So you just gotta hang in there for a couple more days, right? Keep up your sense o' humour and you'll be outta here in no time. Then you can come over to my place.

[ALLAN *chuckles*]

What? What?

ALLAN I dunno if this counts, but I got almost hysterical this morning. They have volleyball, like for the looney tunes here? So I thought I'd go along and check it out. But the ceiling of the room is only eight feet high. So all these drugged-out mental patients are boomphing this Nerf ball into the ceiling. It's sad, eh, but it's just so funny. It's like Holiday on Quaaludes. Me and this chick—I think she's supposed to be manic depressive—we just got hysterical. I thought I was going to piss myself.

JIM So you gonna go back for more?

ALLAN You bet. This chick is beautiful.

JIM Alright.

[*standing*] I gotta go. I got work to do.

[*touching* ALLAN*'s shoulder*] Keep your pecker up.

ALLAN Always.

[*as* JIM *is leaving*] ... Hey. I'm sorry about all this, eh? It never shoulda happened.

JIM Hey. You're my brudda. Shaddup!

[JIM *exits*]

Sleep-Over

RALPH *sits, while* JIM *goes in and out of the room, getting linen for the couch, making it into a bed (for one), etc.*

RALPH I can't believe you think this is a good idea. I mean, he's having a lot of trouble, right? Isn't he violent or something? Wasn't there an assault charge?

JIM Oh, for Christ's sake! There was never any assault charge. He dropped this guy at school 'cause this guy called him a faggot.

RALPH Oh, wonderful! He's gonna love this neighbourhood. Just wait till you have all your friends over for brunch. I wonder how many of us'll be left standing.

JIM He was defending my honour. Al's always tried to punch anybody out who called me a faggot. Now he just hates the word.

RALPH Hmm. Well, I don't think his affection extends to gay men in general. I remember the first time I met him. I don't know how he did it, but he made me feel like I was wearing a dress. And it wasn't very fetching.

[JIM *opens his mouth to speak, but* RALPH *speaks over him*]

   Seriously. I'm worried about you. He's gonna take a lot of energy.

JIM I know. I'm up for it. It's my energy.

RALPH Alright, alright. I just don't know why you always have to be the one to pick up the pieces in your family.

JIM What am I supposed to do, put Allan in a group home? He's seventeen, for Christ's sake. I don't have any other relatives I'd trust to take care of a hamster.

RALPH I just think you should be taking care of yourself.

JIM I'm perfectly healthy, thanks. Admit it. You're just jealous 'cause he's moving in and you've moved out.

RALPH Oh. Psychology. Alright. I am jealous. But I still think this is a stupid thing to do. Okay?

JIM By the way, I'd appreciate the key to the apartment back.

RALPH [*trying to embrace* JIM] Never. Sooner or later you're gonna realize I'm the only one who knows how to fix the toaster.

JIM [*backing off*] Just gimme the key back.

[*Beat*]

RALPH That's the real reason you kicked me out, isn't it? You're afraid to have sex.

JIM Unlike yourself. That's hardly the whole story anyway.

RALPH The other things could be fixed. There is such a thing as safe sex, you know.

JIM Not for me there isn't.

[*Beat*]

RALPH You know what I feel like? Like we're Siamese twins. But you've got this little hacksaw out and you're trying to cut us apart. Like right through the flesh. [*he makes the sound of a tiny saw*]

JIM [*looking at his watch*] I hate to say this. But you gotta go now. Allan's due here any minute.

RALPH And he's not allowed to see the faggot? What? Gimme a coupla minutes and I'll lower my voice.

JIM Don't get like that.

RALPH I've met him already.

JIM And wasn't that a triumph! He's having a hard time, alright? Just let him get used to being here.

RALPH Sure. That's great. Just as long as I know where I stand. It's kind of irresponsible of him, in a way, isn't it? Making all these demands on you when you're sick?

JIM I offered.

RALPH And I'll bet he hardly even knew he was asking. Just wait till you see how many friends he arrives with.

JIM You can shut up anytime.

RALPH Does anybody in your family ever think about how you feel? 'Good ol' Jim. He's always such a soft touch. Who cares if he has AIDS?'

JIM It's not like that.

  Allan doesn't even know I'm sick.

RALPH What? What?

JIM I told my mother. She thought it was better not to tell him and for once I agree with her.

RALPH Are you out of your mind? What's going to happen when he finds out?

JIM I'm going to tell him when I'm good and ready. Got that?

RALPH I'm sure he'll be really honoured to know how much you trust him. Gee, I didn't know you guys were that close.

JIM Butt out.

[*The intercom buzzes*]

  That's him.

RALPH Maybe I should just jump out the window. It's only the fourth floor.

JIM Just be good.

RALPH You mean act straight. [*he buzzes the door open*]

  Maybe we should reconsider the window. I always act like a queen when there are Nazis present, and I think I see a little moustache forming on your upper lip.

[JIM *goes to the door.* ALLAN *and* SHERRI *enter*]

ALLAN Hi.

JIM Oh, hi. Come on in.

RALPH Hi, Al. [*gasps*] What a surprise! You brought a friend.

ALLAN Oh ... yeah ... I hope it's alright. See, Sherri-Lee was just visiting. She didn't know I was getting out. Oh, sorry, Jim this is Sherri-Lee. [*to* SHERRI] This is the guy I told you all about.

JIM Hi.

SHERRI Hi.

[JIM *and* SHERRI *smile at one another. Beat*]

RALPH And I'm Ralph.

JIM Oh. Sorry. Sherri-Lee. This is Ralph. We used to be roommates.

ALLAN Yeah, Jim said you guys ... Like you got your own place, eh?

RALPH Yeah, well, I came home one day and my furniture was on the street. What could I do?

JIM We're still friends.

So sit, sit.

[*as they sit*] You live up the valley, Sherri-Lee?

ALLAN Yeah. Um. Jim? We don't know what we're gonna do, actually. Sherri-Lee took the bus in, but she's missed the last one home.

RALPH [*feigning surprise and concern*] Oh!

SHERRI That's okay. No problem. I got other friends I can stay with. Really.

ALLAN No. Um. We were thinking ... Well, I was thinking ... like ... maybe Sherri-Lee could stay here.

JIM What about your parents?

SHERRI No problem. You can phone my Mom if you want.

ALLAN Yeah. Sherri's Mom's cool.

JIM Well, then ... We'll phone later, eh? Why not? And if it's okay with her, we'll just open out the couch.

ALLAN Alright. Thanks.

RALPH Gee, if I brought my dates home to my brother's, he would've called the police.

JIM You guys want something to drink?

SHERRI Gin an' tonic, if you got it.

285

JIM   Um. Actually I was thinking more along the lines of Perrier and juice.

ALLAN   Sure. That's great.

SHERRI   Fine. I guess it's kinda early anyway. [*to* RALPH] So are you one of the family?

RALPH   Not technically. No.

SHERRI   That's funny. You know, you and Jim look more like brothers than Jim and Al.

RALPH   It's the haircuts.

SHERRI   I guess.

[JIM *arrives back with the drinks*]

Wow, you've got a really nice place. It's just like my apartment's gonna be when I get one. Except I'd probably use more mirrors. You know. Open up the space.

RALPH   Yeah. Well, you know what they say, 'It takes a fairy to make something beautiful.'

[SHERRI *looks at* ALLAN]

JIM   [*to* RALPH] Don't be a dink. [*to* SHERRI] Ralph thinks it's funny to put people on the spot.

RALPH   Sorry.

I'm surprised Allan didn't tell you we were gay, though. We don't embarrass you, do we Al?

JIM   That's enough. Okay?

SHERRI   Actually, I have a friend who said I should get to meet some homosexuals.

RALPH   Really?

SHERRI   Yeah. She said they give the best blowjobs and I could probably pick up some tips.

[*Stunned silence. Then everybody laughs*]

RALPH   I like this girl already!

Doughnuts

JIM *addresses the audience, which acts as his HIV support group throughout the play. This is his first night at the group*

JIM Oh, Christ. My turn, right? Where should I start?
There were lots o' little things—this coating on my tongue, fever, diarrhoea. But that could've been anxiety, right? Then I got this spot. On my chest. It looked like a raisin trying to come through my skin. When I went to the doctor, I wanted him to tell me it wasn't true.

[*Beat*]

I didn't know how to tell Ralph.

[*In* JIM*'s apartment.* RALPH *is sitting at the kitchen table. He's in the dark.* JIM *barges in, carrying a box of doughnuts. He throws them on the counter, and stops suddenly, head down, breathing heavily*]

RALPH Hi.
JIM [*startled*] Jesus Christ! What are you doing home so early?
RALPH I went to visit Luis. Remember? I thought we were both gonna go.
JIM [*flicking on the lights*] I'll never get used to you sitting around in the dark.
RALPH It calms me down.
JIM [*going to the kitchen*] Yeah, well beer calms me down. You want one?

RALPH No thanks. Beer and doughnuts. How *do* you keep your figure?

Luis asked about you. Wanted to know why you hadn't been up.

JIM Tell him I been busy?

RALPH I don't think he buys it.

JIM [*fumbles with the twist cap. He hurts himself*] Shit!

RALPH What's the matter with you?

JIM Ah, it's nothing. I dunno why it upset me so much. People are just jerks, you know. You're right. I should go visit Luis.

RALPH Don't tell me it's nothing. Look at you.

[*Beat*]

Spit it out.

JIM It was stupid. I was just ... I was in Nuffy's picking up— lunch. And there was a bag lady in there, a street person, and she wanted a cup of coffee. She'd probably been panhandling change all morning, but she finally had enough for a cup and she spreads it out on the counter, like it's this big triumph for her ...

RALPH And they won't serve her?

JIM Oh, they serve her, alright. Taking her money is no problem. But they won't let her sit in the restaurant. Like she's going to ruin the *je ne sais quoi* of Nuffy's, for Christ's sake. It's god- damn pouring out and they tell her to take her coffee outside.

RALPH So you come to her rescue.

JIM You know what really pissed me off? The woman who's throwing her out—is Vietnamese. I mean an immigrant woman, working for minimum wage. You'd think she'd know what it feels like to be stepped on. But no, she's got to prove she's better than somebody else. With all the other shit going down ...

RALPH So, what'd you do?

JIM I just emptied my wallet and gave it to the bag lady.

Mark Saunders (**JIM**) and Rob Osborne (**RALPH**)
Photographer: Elisabeth Feryn

RALPH How much?

JIM About forty bucks.

[*They both laugh for a second. Beat*]

[*near tears*] People are just such jerks.

RALPH What else?

JIM [*shakes his head*] That's it.

RALPH I can't say I feel much better myself. Luis can hardly see out his left eye. The Kaposi's is all over his face. You remember Daniel? He used to be Leonard's lover.

[JIM *nods*]

He died.
It's like a tidal wave, you know. Sometimes I wonder if there's going to be anybody left. You know my biggest fear? That I'm gonna be the last faggot. Scary, eh? It'd be like moving back to Thunder Bay.

[RALPH *smiles at* JIM *and touches his leg*]

We've gotta stick together, okay? Let's make that a deal.

[*Beat*]

JIM You know what?
I think I've already blown it.

RALPH What?

JIM I didn't know how to tell you.

RALPH Tell me what? Come on, Jimmy, don't screw around.

JIM I've got it.

[*Beat*]

RALPH Did you get tested?

[JIM *nods*]

Just because you tested positive doesn't mean ...
JIM I haven't just tested positive.

[*Beat.* JIM *rolls up his shirt and reveals a small lesion*]

It won't go away.

[RALPH *looks at the lesion and looks away. Beat*]

RALPH Have they done a biopsy?
JIM Yes.
RALPH Spots can be anything, you know. Remember that
time I got a flea bite from Gerry's cat? I was scared to death.
Remember that? I kept finding them all over my body. Spots
can be anything.
JIM [*looks at* RALPH] I've been tested. Twice.

[*Beat*]

RALPH Why didn't you tell me?
[*beat*] How long have you known, or like, suspected?
JIM I dunno ...
RALPH Why didn't you tell me? I mean I knew something was
going on. But I never thought ...
JIM I tried. But I been so scared. It was like, if I said it, it would
all of a sudden be true. I've been afraid to do anything. I been
afraid to breathe.

[*Beat*]

RALPH C'mere.

[RALPH *tries to touch* JIM. JIM *pulls away*]

JIM Don't. Okay?
RALPH Why not?
If we stick together, we can handle this.
JIM [*with a laugh*] Yeah. Sure. Maybe you can handle it.

I'm experiencing a slight technical difficulty.

I'm sure you'll be fine, though. Don't ask me how. I just know.

RALPH Who cares about me?

JIM [*suddenly angry*] I do! Don't you ever say anything so stupid.

RALPH Okay, okay. I didn't mean it like that.

JIM [*drops his gaze to the floor*] I made an appointment for you next week.

RALPH Yeah.

Okay.

Come on.

[JIM *shakes his head. Beat*]

There's new drugs all the time, you know.

JIM Yeah.

RALPH People live because they want to live. I've seen it.

You saw Patrick. Everybody thought he was at death's door.

JIM Do me a favour, okay? Don't lecture me.

RALPH Right. 'Cause you've decided you're the one who's sick and I'm the one who gets left behind. Well, it's not gonna be that easy. You better live. You better want to live, goddammit. 'Cause this isn't just your little life, alright? You're my other half.

JIM [*addresses the audience/support group*] Ralph tested negative a couple of weeks after that. I hosted a smart champagne brunch, but Ralph was depressed, almost like he was embarrassed by his health. The second person I told was my mother.

End Time

JIM [*addresses the audience/support group*] I wrote her a letter. 'Cause I couldn't face telling her in person. You know what I got back?

[*reads from his mother's letter*] 'Jim, my precious son. Meditate and forgive me for being your mother.'

Snappy opener.

'I know you don't want me to lecture you, and this will be the last time I will do it, but I have a right. I am your mother, and in pain did I bear you.' [*a short laugh from* JIM]

'The sexual revolution came about when man chose to ignore God's laws, but now we are paying the wages of sin. Our pastor says that we are in the end time. We can see the signs: fish dying in our lakes, earthquakes, famine, and war, as foretold in Revelations. And AIDS is that last plague.'

[*he turns the page*] 'You must not think this means I do not love you. I do. Perhaps my greatest fault was loving you too much, but you were always a sickly child, even born without toenails as my resources were so depleted at the time.'

[*he laughs and holds up his hands to show off his fingernails*] They grew in.

'And now the doctors say that homosexuality is always the mother's fault. How do you think that makes me feel, now that you are so sick? Not good I can tell you.'

[*to the group*] Like, when I was little, I was home, sick, and we couldn't find my paintbrush, and so she made me one out of a pencil and a chunk of her hair.

And I know it sounds stupid, but some part of me … still hoped. Like, you know, she was still gonna be the one. To take care o' me.

[*he reads*] 'I have enclosed some pamphlets and a sample of the new wallpaper in the bathroom. The theme is rose and spring green. Read James 4 and 5. Expect a miracle as I do. I love you, Mom.'

[*he dumps out the wallpaper sample and holds it up*] She did, too. I don't know if I'd call that spring green, though. More of a sage, don't you think?

Whoopsi

During the transition into this scene, ALLAN *is drinking beer in his playing area. He may have entered and started to drink at the beginning of 'End Time'*

In JIM*'s apartment, the sofa bed is out. Dim light.* JIM *is sitting on the edge of the bed. He's in his underwear and has a towel around his neck.* JIM *moans and puts his head in his hands*

ALLAN *sneaks in the door*

JIM Where've you been?
ALLAN Nowhere. Out.
　　What're you doin' up?
JIM I don't feel so good.
ALLAN So go back to bed then.
JIM You been drinking?
ALLAN No.
JIM Sure?
ALLAN Yeah. What? You wanna smell my breath?

[*Beat*]

JIM Yeah.
ALLAN I been dry as a bone since I been here.
JIM You were supposed to be back by midnight.
ALLAN Well, maybe you just shoulda had the cops tail me.
JIM [*shakes his head*] I can smell it from here.
ALLAN So what? So I had a couple beers. Hours ago.

JIM A coupla beers! I thought we had a deal. 'One beer an' I'm
out.' Wasn't that it?

ALLAN So one little slip. It's not like I got drunk or anything.
It's just a couple beers. I can handle it now. In the old days,
I woulda come home blind drunk.

JIM [*standing and applauding*] Congratulations! You didn't come
home blind drunk! Just a little pissed and then you lie to me.

ALLAN Okay! So whaddyou want? I'll move out. Is that what you
want? I'll move out.

JIM [*quietly*] Oh shit. [*he collapses*]

ALLAN What ...?

Jim! What the hell? Are you alright, man?

[ALLAN *tries to lift him up*]

Jesus! You're soaking wet.

JIM Don't do that. I'm gonna be sick.

Oh. I do not feel too good.

ALLAN What's going on? You want me to call a doctor?

JIM No. No. Just let me get back up onto the bed and bring me
a bowl.

[ALLAN *hoists* JIM *onto the day-bed, where* JIM *sits with his head
between his knees.* ALLAN *gets a small bowl*]

I think I can do better than that.

[ALLAN *gets a large, stainless-steel bowl*]

Thanks.

I had a bug a while back. Just can't get rid of it. Sorry.

ALLAN What have you got to be sorry about?

JIM Nothing. Christ.

ALLAN You okay?

JIM Yeah. Just stay here a second, okay?

ALLAN Yeah.

[*Beat*]

JIM You shouldn't be drinking.
ALLAN Geez! Give it a rest!

[*Beat*]

JIM You can do it, alright?
    I just wanna be proud of ya.

[*Beat*]

ALLAN Yeah.
    Hey. 'Member when we were kids? I was the barf champion.
    You used to come and hold my head and tell me the plots of
    old TV shows.
JIM Yeah.
ALLAN 'Member that time when I had mumps or something?
    Mom didn't want you in the room 'cause they were catching.
    But I screamed till she let you in.
JIM [*laughs*] I told you a whole summer's worth of 'Gilligan's
    Island.'
    [*suddenly about to vomit*] Whoopsi!

[JIM *leans over the bowl and* ALLAN *holds his forehead. They
wait*]

ALLAN You gonna throw up?
JIM Not yet.
ALLAN You wanna go back to bed?
JIM In a minute. I gotta change the sheets. I woke up drenched.
ALLAN You want me to change 'em?
JIM That's okay. I'll do it myself. In a minute.
    Oh, this is the shits. I feel like I'm falling.
    Seen any good TV lately?
ALLAN Only dirty videos.

JIM Tell me the story.

ALLAN They're straight.

JIM Well then, forget it. I already feel sick to my stomach.

[*They wait*]

ALLAN How ya doin'?

JIM It's not gonna happen. You prob'ly want your bed now, right? That's okay. I think I better lie down.

[JIM *picks up the bowl and stands*]

ALLAN You gonna be okay?

JIM I think so, yeah.

ALLAN You don't sound too sure.

JIM [*heading towards the bedroom*] Don't worry about it. I'll be okay.

[*without turning around,* JIM *waves a hand*] I just wanna be proud of you, alright?

[JIM *exits*]

ALLAN Yeah.

[ALLAN *lies down on the bed, then notices that the sheets are soaked. He strips the bed*]

Shit Happens

Having changed into his street clothes, JIM *approaches the front of the stage. He's still in his first night at group. He listens to somebody else, then responds to them*

JIM   Yeah. Okay. What I'm feeling in my body? Okay. A bit like throwing up, actually. An' I guess that's 'cause I was scared shitless about coming here tonight. Yeah. I had to put my hand on the door handle three times before I could open it. And then I just had to count to ten and do it. I never been involved in a gay organization before.

[*He is interrupted*]

   Well, I was in shock for about two months, but I think that's finally starting to turn around.

[*Question*]

   Well, it was ... I was out for a walk with my friend Ralph. And we'd been having a pretty good day, actually. He hadn't been trying to get into my pants or anything, which is his favourite occupation. He's my ex. But he hadn't been trying to do that. So we were just walking along the sea wall and I started to get—I don't know if you ever get like this, but I started to hate the healthy. You know what I mean? Yeah. So I was starting to hate the healthy, which takes a lot of energy, so we had to sit down. And then this little girl comes running along. Can't be more than about eighteen months.

Not really talking yet. But she sees us and her face just lights up. Like we're the people she's been looking for all day. And then I notice that she's only got one and a half arms. Like her right arm is just this little flipper thing. And the fingers are like toes. But she doesn't care—they're wiggling away. And in a split second, I go from thinking, 'Why me?' to, 'Why her?' What'd she ever do to anybody? And I'm just getting all fired up about this when her father comes running up to grab her. You know what his T-shirt says? 'Shit happens'!

'Shit happens.' It was like a revelation. Like these guys are a one-two punch from heaven. And then! And then! This is the weirdest part. This little kid says, 'It isn't raining!' Just like that. 'It isn't raining!' Like this is the secret we've all been waiting for. And she says it right to me.

Like we've all gotta live until we die, right?

[*Question*]

I guess my biggest problem now is guilt. Yeah. I told my mother. She's born again, right? I have a brother, too. I feel like … in my case, I just feel like I deserve it.

Perfect Music

ALLAN *and* SHERRI *are in the sofa bed in* JIM'*s apartment. It's almost dawn*

SHERRI So, on that first night, how come you never told me he was gay? I felt like a complete loser.

ALLAN 'Cause he's not gay. To me. He's not. Now, Ralph. Ralph's a fag. But Jim's not. I don't care what they do in bed, just so long's they don't go wavin' a flag about it.

SHERRI Oh, look. Lookit the sky. I love it when the sky does that.

[SHERRI *kneels up on the bed so she can see out the window*]

ALLAN What?

SHERRI C'mere.

[*She drags him up*]

ALLAN Oh, yeah. Sun's comin' up.

SHERRI Yeah, but look. Like on that apartment building over there. Incredible colours, eh? This is gonna sound stupid, but doesn't it look like the sun's rubbing up against that building? Like she's rubbing her body up against him? [*she looks at* ALLAN *and smiles*]

ALLAN Yeah.

SHERRI It's like she's turning all the cold purple spots to orange. And it's like the trees are all still wet and dark from the rain. Like they're just shivering and they just can't wait for their turn!

ALLAN [*laughs*] That's the kinda shit Jim's always coming up with. I know what you mean, though. I do.

SHERRI I know you do.

[*They kiss*]

I'm glad you're not like anybody else.

ALLAN Just a sec. Just a sec.

[*He pulls himself away from her and starts flipping through a pile of tapes*]

SHERRI What're you doing?

ALLAN My turn.

[*He flips on a recording of the soprano Montserrat Caballé*]

SHERRI What's that?

[ALLAN *returns to her and hugs her from behind. They're both kneeling again, looking out the window*]

ALLAN Perfect music.

SHERRI I never liked opera.

ALLAN Shut up and listen for a sec.

[*They listen. It's the aria 'Vissi d'Arte, Vissi d'Amore,' from* Tosca]

I never liked it either. But Jim made me listen. Practically had to tie me down. But he told me it's not a snob thing. It's just like the sun coming up. It's just there for everybody. Can you hear it?

SHERRI Mm. What's she singing about?

ALLAN 'Bout how she lived her whole life for love.

SHERRI Nice work if you can get it.

[SHERRI *pulls away from* ALLAN *and sits on the bed.* ALLAN *takes her hand*]

ALLAN I been thinking. Next year when we finish school an' that. *If* I finish school an' that. An' if we can get jobs. Maybe we should think about moving into the city here.

SHERRI You mean, like, together?

ALLAN Of course, like together! Whaddyou think, we're gonna live in different neighbourhoods?

SHERRI I dunno.
     [*beat*] I dunno. I already promised Heather I'd move into the city with her and we'd try and get jobs in the same place.

ALLAN Yeah, okay. It's stupid. I was just thinkin' about it.

[SHERRI *puts her hand on* ALLAN*'s*]

SHERRI Maybe. Maybe we should think about it.
     [*beat*] I've had lots of boyfriends.
     Whlaa! [*she makes a sound and a face*]

ALLAN What?

SHERRI I just feel so stupid saying this. I've had lots of boy-friends, but ... But it's like most of them don't even see me. They just see my clothes or my hair or something. Or my tits. But you're different. You're the world's softest kisser for one thing. And you're the first one I really loved.

[SHERRI *laughs, embarrassed. She puts her hands to her face*]

ALLAN What? What? Am I that ugly lookin' you have to be embarrassed by what you just said?

SHERRI No.

ALLAN Alright, then, look at me.

[*She looks up at him and* ALLAN *holds* SHERRI*'s face in his hands*]

     I love you, too.

[*He kisses her, very softly*]

     Dawn's a funny time, isn't it?

SHERRI Whaddyou mean?

ALLAN Like there's a whole new day out there. But all of a sudden, I'm just ... really lonely. Like for everything.

No Fluids

Daytime in JIM*'s apartment.* JIM *is about to leave*

RALPH Just a minute. Just a minute. You have to hear this.

[*He slips a tape into the tape deck. The tape plays Klaus Nomi or some other operatic disco queen*]

The voice.

JIM Amazing control, eh?

RALPH Just a second. He's gonna blast your ears off.

[*The singer's volume suddenly increases*]

JIM Holy shit! Wouldn't it be great to open your mouth and have that come out!

RALPH No problem. [*he starts to sing along in a horrible falsetto*]

JIM Spare me! Dub it for me, would ya? I gotta go pick up Al.

RALPH Let him take care of himself.

JIM What?

RALPH [*turning off the tape deck*] I've hardly seen you for three weeks. I bring over a new tape and everything. And bingo, you wanna take off! What'd I do?

JIM Nothing.

RALPH Fine. Don't let me keep you.

JIM Are you alright?

RALPH Not actually. No.

[JIM *is instantly concerned*]

Don't worry. Just lonely.
I've got this mildly embarrassing favour to ask.
Would you mind holding me for a sec?
[*anticipating* JIM'*s protest, holding up his hands*] Just a hug.
No fluids.

[JIM *wraps his arms around* RALPH. RALPH *makes the most of it*]

I've tried developing relationships with stuffed animals, but
they aren't working out.
[*he pulls his head back so he can look at* JIM] Don't you miss
this?
JIM Yes. Alright?
Enough?
RALPH Of course not. But that's life.

[JIM *gives* RALPH *a squeeze and releases him.* JIM *sits on the sofa.*
RALPH *also sits, but not too near* JIM]

So. Whaddyou do for sex these days? Just a survey question.
JIM [*holding up his hand*] Mary Five-Fingers. We're engaged.
RALPH [*nods*] Well, I'm free to pick up on all those offers I had
when we were married.
This guy followed me home from the Aquatic Centre the
other day. Body-builder. He felt like rubber, though. Like the
Michelin man.
JIM [*hangs his head*] I wish you wouldn't. Sex just scares me.
All of it.

[RALPH *touches* JIM *lightly*]

RALPH Remember what it used to be like? When you first discovered fucking? It was like once I gave myself permission, I
couldn't say no. It was like stopping myself would've been a
crime or something.
JIM Yeah. Maybe what we were doing was the crime.

RALPH Who's that, your mother talking? Nobody knew. Look at me.

[JIM *looks at* RALPH]

Nobody knew.

I think you should be having sex. Celibacy isn't natural at your age.

You know what I think? I think Allan's provided you with a perfect little walk-in closet.

He arrived at just the right time, didn't he? You're freaked out about sex, so now you can devote your time to being that little delinquent's daddy.

JIM Fascinating theory, but it's none of your business.

RALPH I know what it was like when you were growing up.

JIM Oh, you do, eh?

RALPH Yeah. What you told me. Your father was a maniac.

JIM You don't know Allan.

RALPH I know what I see.

JIM Drop it, alright? Allan needs me. [*he tosses back a pill*]

RALPH Sure he does. But you can't be his big brother forever.

[*Beat*]

JIM Is that what you're trying to tell me? Because I'm sick, I'm supposed to start letting him go?

RALPH I didn't mean it like ...

JIM [*interrupting*] Well, fuck you! Allan needs me. You have no idea what it was like.

RALPH Okay, okay. I'm just saying ...

JIM Well, keep it to yourself! It wasn't like your family, okay? The fucking Brady Bunch!

[*beat*] Our dad ... Did I ever tell you about the day he tried to kill us? He was playing with a gun, alright? Just horsing around, but he was drunk and it went off. The bullet went

into the wall about an inch and a half above my head. Allan was screaming. My mom was screaming. It was pretty wild.

[*Beat*]

RALPH What'd you do?

JIM I just walked across the room to him. And he just went all soft and gave the gun to me, like I was a little cop.

RALPH And you've been the family cop ever since.

JIM Fuck you.

RALPH But you can't have sex with Allan, can ya?

JIM Am I missing something in this conversation? What are you talking about? He's my brother for Christ's sake.

RALPH And you're afraid of what he'd think if he knew you had sex with anybody else.

JIM He knows I'm gay.

RALPH And he knows nuns have vaginas. They're just not supposed to use them. He thinks being gay's alright, just so long's you don't do it. That's why you don't want to tell him you're sick, isn't it? Proof of sex.

[*Pause*]

JIM Maybe.
     [*short pause*] I found my dad once, you know. In a bar down along Pender. It was like he didn't even know me. I mean it was pretty obvious he didn't want to remember, right?

RALPH Why'd you go looking for him?

JIM You're the one with all the answers. To ask him why he tried to kill me?

RALPH Whaddyou figure?

JIM I really don't know. Something about me. Being gay.

RALPH Allan's like him, isn't he? Is that why you're afraid to tell Allan you have AIDS?

JIM Maybe.

307

[RALPH *leans over and puts his hand on the nape of* JIM *'s neck*]

RALPH If he loves you, he'll hang in there.

JIM I want to tell him, but it's like ... when I think about it, it's like I'm ashamed.

RALPH You haven't done anything to be ashamed of. You're a beautiful man.

[RALPH *picks up* JIM *'s hand and kisses his fingers*]

JIM It's like if I hadn't been gay ...

[RALPH *puts a finger to* JIM *'s lips to silence him.* JIM *takes* RALPH *'s hand and holds it*]

RALPH If you hadn't been gay, you wouldn't have survived. Neither would he. Allan loves you for who you are.

    You haven't done anything wrong. You should be proud of yourself.

[RALPH *picks up both of* JIM *'s hands and kisses them*]

Tea for Three

JIM *is at his support group again, but this meeting takes place some time after his first night*

JIM My mother came for a visit. She wanted Allan back.

Like right away she starts going on about how I'm not providing him with the proper Christian influence. But we all know what that means, right? Like she's afraid she's gonna end up with another little faggot. Like living with me's gonna turn Al gay, for Christ's sake. But she doesn't want to say it out loud, just in case she turns into a pillar of salt. And when I start to push her on that, she says, 'Tell Allan the truth about your flu.' She says, 'Allan's got a right to know the truth.' Christ. Like he's gonna catch it from the fuckin' toilet seat.

[JIM *barges into the living-room.* ALLAN *is already there*]

ALLAN What the hell's going on?

[JIM *ignores* ALLAN]

What was that all about?

JIM [*shaking his head*] Nothing. I just wish she'd mind her own goddamn business, that's all.

ALLAN What was she talking about?

JIM She just wants you back with her, that's all.

ALLAN Well, fuck that. I'm not goin' back. Fuck that, right? [*beat*] Right?

JIM I dunno.

It's not working out that great here.

ALLAN Whaddyou mean?

JIM [*clearing away tea things*] Your drinking for one thing.

ALLAN [*suddenly helping with the clean-up*] No but really. That's really under control. Really. Not another drop.

JIM Yeah, but the real thing is ... I'm just not shaking this flu, eh? Maybe it's Epstein-Barr or something, but I'm not shakin' it. So I been thinking about going on disability for a while. I might have to move into a smaller place.

ALLAN No, but that's okay. That's okay, see? 'Cause I been thinking about getting a job anyway. Whaddyou think, I was just gonna sponge off you for the rest of my life? No way! I got a job all lined up and everything. Well, I'm pretty sure I could get it. It's good pay, man. Doin' deliveries an' that.

JIM What about school?

[*Beat*]

ALLAN Forget school.

Forget it. I mean I gotta work full time if I'm gonna make any real money, right?

JIM Don't be stupid. You've got to finish school.

ALLAN I don't *have* to do anything.

JIM Well, you gotta finish school, an' that's that. You're not gonna throw yourself away on some dead-end delivery job.

ALLAN Hey, you ever notice how much you sound like her? Really. That's what she always used to say about you, 'I don't know why Jim's throwing himself away on word processing. When he was a child, he was such an artist.' It was like everything you produced—your turds should be in museums!

[*beat*] Right? You're just like her. That's why you guys always get so wired when you're together.

I never seen you get so pissed off at her, though. You practically threw her out.

[*Beat*]

JIM Yeah.

[*Beat*]

ALLAN So what'd she mean about your flu?
    Come on.
    You trying to get rid of me or what?
JIM No! I just ...
ALLAN Well, what's she talkin' about?

[*Beat*]

JIM I've always tried to take care of ya. Ya know that, right?
    I mean I was just a kid, so I guess I couldn't be the world's best
    dad ...

[*Beat*]

ALLAN What are *you* talkin' about?
JIM I'm sick.

[*Beat.* JIM *looks at* ALLAN. *He doesn't know what to say*]

ALLAN Count to ten.

[*Beat*]

JIM I have AIDS.
    [*beat*] I got KS—that's a kind of cancer—about six months
    ago. I was sick—little things—for a while before that.

[*Beat*]

ALLAN So why didn't you tell me?

[JIM *shakes his head*]

    Oh man, what's wrong with me? What's wrong with me?

You ... you're sick, and I didn't even know? You didn't even
tell?

JIM I didn't ...

ALLAN I guess Ralph knows, right? I guess everybody else knows.
I guess you figured I couldn't take it. I guess you must think
I'm a real fuck-up.

JIM Take it easy. I know it's a shock.

[*Pause*]

ALLAN So why can't I stay with you? I could still stay with you.

[JIM *looks at* ALLAN]

No, it'd be good, 'cause I could help, right?
Besides, that's the way it's always been. You an' me, right?

JIM No. You don't know what this means.

ALLAN You think I'm stupid? You think I don't know what this
means?
I know what it means and I wanna stay with you. Like you
always done everything for me, right?
Let me.
How sick are you? Like right now?

JIM [*shrugs*] You been here. Good days. Bad days. It's no big deal.

[*Beat*]

ALLAN So? What do the doctors say? Like ...

JIM Years maybe. A long time.

ALLAN Yeah? Yeah? So?
You're not gonna get rid o' me, ya know.
Are you okay? Like right this minute?

JIM Yeah, I'm fine. I'm good.
There's no danger to you, either. From being here.

ALLAN I'm staying with you, man. You can't kick me out. You'd
hafta call the cops.

[*Beat*]

JIM Okay, maybe. Maybe. We can see how it goes, eh?

Ya wanna know something weird about having AIDS? It's like it really clears up your TV set. It's sort of like everything used to have some sort of filter on it before. But I can see you so clear right now. And Technicolor. You wouldn't believe how beautiful you look.

Baggy

In the transition into this scene **ALLAN** *is in his playing area, smoking a joint*

As the lights come up on **JIM**'*s apartment,* **RALPH** *and* **JIM** *are on the sofa,* **RALPH** *massaging* **JIM**'*s feet.* **JIM** *moans, then screams.* **RALPH** *shows no mercy. They fight and giggle*

ALLAN *enters from outside, carrying his knapsack.* **JIM** *immediately swings his feet away from* **RALPH**

ALLAN [*to* **JIM**, *ignoring* **RALPH**] How you doing?

JIM Great.

ALLAN I picked up some groceries.

JIM What'd you get?

ALLAN All that health-food shit you asked for.
     [*he takes out a fresh joint*] And a little medicine of my own.
     [*to* **RALPH**] You gave me the idea, actually. Sort of.

JIM Dope?

ALLAN Anti-nausea medication. Shut up before you even say it.
     It'll be good for both of us. [*to* **RALPH**] They use it in hospitals
     an' that, right? For medical purposes. That's what you said.

RALPH Yeah, I said that, but ...

ALLAN [*interrupting. To* **JIM**] Let's put it this way—is anything
     else making you feel any better?

JIM No.

ALLAN Alright, then. Have a toke.

     [**ALLAN** *lights the joint and hands it to* **JIM**. **JIM** *puts it out*]

JIM Thanks. But no thanks.

ALLAN Well …! What about me, man?

JIM Forget it. It's for medical purposes, right? I think I'll save it till later.

ALLAN Yeah, but …! I bought it!

JIM I can't have you smoking dope in the house. Have you got any more?

ALLAN No!

[JIM *pulls a baggy out of* ALLAN*'s knapsack*]

I paid for that!

JIM Shoulda known better. Grow up. It's only a joint.

RALPH I just sort of mentioned it as an interesting medical fact. Sorry.

[*Beat.* ALLAN *is furious*]

JIM Don't feel too bad. I asked Ralph to pick up a couple o' things for you and Sherri-Lee today. She's coming in again this weekend, right? Well, I got a whole new wardrobe for you. I stuffed it in your jacket pocket.

[ALLAN *looks from* RALPH *to* JIM]

Go ahead. I asked him to pick them up. We were talking about it.

ALLAN [*goes over to his jacket*] What is this? Safes?

JIM Yeah. They come in six tropical colours. Just think how much fun you'll have trying them on. I don't know what size you want, but Ralph says one size fits all.

[ALLAN *shakes his head. He is furious*]

What's the matter?

ALLAN [*throwing the condoms at* RALPH] Fuck you.

JIM What was that?

315

ALLAN Fuck you! I get the point, alright? But I can take care of
myself.

JIM You use safes every time?

ALLAN What?

JIM You heard me.

ALLAN Who're you, the sex police?

JIM Do you?

ALLAN Yes! Alright? Yes! I laminate myself for Chrissake!

[*Beat*]

JIM You know why I'm asking.

ALLAN Yeah.

JIM Ralph was talking to Sherri-Lee.

ALLAN Oh, fuck you! Fuck you both!

[ALLAN *storms off. Beat*]

RALPH Well, that went well, don't you think?
Why'd you do that? In front of me?

JIM Why shouldn't I? He's got to know.

RALPH Yeah, but not in front of the dreaded homo.
What's the hurry?

[JIM *shakes his head*]

What's the hurry?

JIM Just a feeling. I wanna get things done, that's all.

A Little Shovel

ALLAN *and* JIM *are sitting at the table*

JIM There's one more thing I wanna ask ya about.

ALLAN Great.

JIM Now don't freak out. I wanna talk about my funeral.

ALLAN Sure, why not? When would you like to have it? Maybe
I should just go out and buy a little shovel right now.

JIM Forget it. I'm gonna be cremated. And I don't want my ashes
to be buried, anyway. There's this place up on the north end
of Vancouver Island where me and Ralph went camping once.
It's called Robson Bight. I already talked to Ralph about it.
So I want you and him to charter one of the boats up there ...

ALLAN Okay, okay.

JIM And sprinkle me on the water.

ALLAN Okay.

JIM And make sure that you're standing upwind when you take
the top off the jar.

[ALLAN *looks at* JIM]

So I don't blow back in your face. I wouldn't want to go up
your nose.

ALLAN Jesus, Jim!

JIM Well, it can happen, you know. I know somebody who was
releasing their lover's ashes. Went straight up his nose. Into his
eyes and everything. This guy said he couldn't blow his nose
for weeks without seeing his friend all over the handerkerchief.

[ALLAN *shakes his head. He starts to head into the back room*]

Don't go in there.

ALLAN Why not?

JIM My stomach. I had the shits before. I couldn't get it all cleaned up.

[*Beat*]

ALLAN You taking your medication?

JIM Yeah. They can't seem to control it.

Just stay outta there. I'll clean it up later.

ALLAN Shut up. I'll get it.

JIM No way! First person who does that's gonna be a nurse.

[*Beat*]

ALLAN Don't be stupid. Where's the Lysol?

JIM Under the sink. Al?

[ALLAN *stops*]

Robson Bight, okay?

I already talked to Ralph about it.

ALLAN [*still with his back to* JIM] Yeah. Yeah. Alright.

Burning

JIM *is at his support group. This is another night*

JIM   I've been keeping all my mother's letters. I don't know why. It's like ... it's this file I have on her or something.

I guess I always wanted proof.

But now, all of a sudden, I don't ... you know ... I don't wanna, like, leave them behind. I guess I don't want other people to read them. I guess all that ... was just between her and me. You know?

But I don't want to throw them out either, like they were nothing. So Ralph says, 'Why don't you burn them?' And I think that's a good idea ... like ... [*laughing*] it's like they're gonna have their own funeral, you know?

[*He sets fire to one of the letters, drops it, and watches it burn*]

I miss her so much.
This feels okay, I guess, but it's not enough.
I wish ... I just wish I could break them.

[*He lights another letter*]

But this is better than nothing.

No Glove, No Love

Music. ALLAN *is on top of* SHERRI, *forcing himself on her*

SHERRI Don't! What's the matter with you?

ALLAN Nothing. What's the matter with you?

SHERRI Where's Jim?

ALLAN He's over at group, that support thing. I'm pickin' him up after.

[*He's on her again. She pushes him off*]

SHERRI Fuck off!

ALLAN What? What's the matter? You don't wanna go around with me any more? You found somebody else? What?

SHERRI What's going on with you?

ALLAN I've missed you, alright? We haven't been alone for a while.

SHERRI I thought you might wanna talk first. What's this 'Me Tarzan' bullshit?

ALLAN Alright. Alright. Just one kiss, then. One kiss. No hands! Look, I'm tying my hands behind my back. Alright? I'm your prisoner.

SHERRI [*laughing*] You're crazy.

ALLAN That's right. I'm your crazy love slave. Dying for one kiss. Just give me one kiss. Right here. A sweet one. Softly.

[SHERRI *kisses him. He immediately takes his hands from behind his back and wraps them around* SHERRI*'s waist. His lovemaking gets passionate*]

SHERRI What's got into you?

ALLAN Nothing. Come on.

[*He pulls* SHERRI *down onto the bed with him*]

SHERRI Allan! I feel like I'm being run over by a Mack truck. You got protection?

[ALLAN *pulls out a safe. He shows it to* SHERRI, *then throws it over his shoulder*]

Allan!

ALLAN I wanna be close to you tonight.

SHERRI So go pick up the safe and we'll be close.

ALLAN Why? I mean really. Why? I mean, you got other protection, right? I mean you said you were already on the pill an' that.

SHERRI Yeah, but the pill's not gonna protect us from AIDS.

ALLAN Listen. Listen. Touch my face.

[SHERRI *hesitates*]

Go ahead. Just touch it.

[*She does. She lingers.* ALLAN *catches one of her fingers in his mouth and sucks it*]

Now imagine doing that with rubber gloves.

SHERRI I can't believe you're talking like this. What about Jimmy?

ALLAN What about Jimmy?

I'm sick and tired of bloody Jimmy, alright? Jim has nothing to do with us. Is he in the room here, huh?

SHERRI He's your brother.

ALLAN What's that supposed to mean?

All the time I was growing up I got that, 'Hey, Anderson, are you a fag, just like your fag brother?' Well, he's gay and

I'm straight, alright?

SHERRI That's not what I'm talking about.

ALLAN What? Did you have sex with him or something? 'Cause I sure as hell didn't.

You're just as paranoid as he is.

SHERRI He's living right here. How can you ignore the fact that he's sick?

ALLAN I know he's sick, alright?

You don't have to remind me about that.

I don't know about you, but this death trip doesn't really turn me on, you know? Just once. Just once, I'd like to have sex without thinking about Jim, okay?

SHERRI Some of those jerks you used to hang around with, they did really heavy drugs before.

ALLAN Oh, yeah, sure. They're not junkies or nothing. I never had sex with nobody who used needles.

SHERRI But how do you know who they had sex with?

ALLAN Fine. Fine. I don't even feel like it any more. You mind if I just go jerk off?

SHERRI Allan! Come on! I'm just trying to be safe.

[*Beat*]

ALLAN We didn't always use rubbers before. I mean sometimes, but ...

SHERRI That was before.

ALLAN Right.

So who you been talkin' to besides Ralph?

I really appreciated that, you know. I mean this fag knows all about our sex life. He even goes out and buys me a pack of safes for Christ's sake. I couldn't use one o' those things. Not after he's been all over 'em.

SHERRI [*lets out a short laugh*] Kinda like having his hands on your dick, eh?

Amanda Stepto (SHERRI-LEE) and David Orth (ALLAN)
Photographer: Elisabeth Feryn

I like Ralph, okay? And he was just tryin' to help.

ALLAN Well, it's none of his business. And I didn't appreciate it.

SHERRI I mean it's not like I'm just gonna get pregnant, you know. Ralph said more girls my age are gettin' it all the time. And we're gettin' it from sex.

[*Beat*]

ALLAN So ... What? You think you're gonna get it from me? Come on. I mean, whatever we got from one another we already got, right? I mean, we're not having sex with other people. Right? We're probably gonna get married.

SHERRI Maybe you are. I'm not.

ALLAN Alright, forget it. I thought we had something special. But hey, you know, I guess I was wrong.

SHERRI Allan! You know how I feel about you.

ALLAN Yeah, I guess I do. You think I got AIDS just 'cause I'm his brother.

SHERRI Don't be stupid! Don't be stupid.

[SHERRI *smooths her fingers through his hair*]

ALLAN I'm trying not to.

[ALLAN *responds. They start to kiss and touch*]

I'm just trying to figure out ... what the big deal is. I mean, we've been going out for months.
[*beat*] I never told anybody else I loved them before.

[ALLAN *continues to kiss and touch* SHERRI. *She pulls back*]

SHERRI Ralph didn't get sick. But he could have. We still could.

[SHERRI *turns away and holds herself*]

ALLAN What? What's the matter?

SHERRI I just feel cold, that's all. My teeth are chattering.

What if I said I love you but I want to use a safe?

ALLAN I'd wanna know why you don't trust me.

SHERRI What's going on with you?

ALLAN Or what you're tryin' to hide.

SHERRI Nothing! I trust you more than any other guy I've ever met. All those other guys ...

ALLAN Well, I'm not those other guys.

    I love you.

[*Their lovemaking gets more passionate throughout the following exchange*]

SHERRI Do you?

ALLAN Yes.

SHERRI Do you really?

ALLAN Yes.

SHERRI So what's the big deal about not using a safe?

ALLAN I wanna feel you. All of you. What's so dangerous?

SHERRI But Jimmy ...

ALLAN I'm not Jimmy. Jim's got nothing to do with us.

SHERRI Are you always gonna be the one?

ALLAN You know I am.

Party

ALLAN *is alone in the apartment. He's drinking, and he has the tape deck cranked up really high.* JIM *enters, noticeably fatigued*

JIM   What the hell's going on here?

ALLAN   Private party.

[JIM *turns the tape deck off and heads towards the table to get his pills*]

JIM   In the middle of the afternoon? This is the last thing I need. My beeper went off and I didn't have my pills. I've got to get back to work.

[ALLAN *cranks the tape deck back up.* JIM *takes his pills with some water*]

ALLAN   Come on. Aren't you goin' to talk to me?

JIM   Why the hell should I talk to you? You're bloody drunk. I thought we had a deal.

ALLAN   Oh, yeah. The big deal. You ever notice you're always tellin' people what to do?

JIM   [*turns the tape deck off again*] What's this all about, huh? What's it all about?

[JIM *sits*]

ALLAN   Aren't you gonna kick me out? Go ahead and kick me out! That'd be great. Sherri-Lee left already. She's really pissed off.

326

JIM You guys fight?

ALLAN No. We just ... you know, we just had sex. [*laughs*]
I hadn't seen her for a while, eh? But then she started gettin' all
weird after. Like really weird. Like she kept sayin' she was cold
an' that. I don't think she's comin' back.

I don't think she really knows ... like what it's like ...

JIM What are you talking about?

ALLAN Well, sometimes you've just got to ... I think she's pissed
off 'cause we didn't use a safe.

JIM What?

ALLAN [*laughing*] I like that. 'What?'

JIM Don't screw around. Are you kidding me?

ALLAN No. Why the hell should we?

And you can stop tellin' me what to do anytime. You're not
the bloody Gestapo, you know. And you're not my old man,
either. You're just my fuckin' brother.

JIM I've never hit you, have I?

ALLAN No.

[JIM *slaps* ALLAN *across the face*]

JIM Don't you ever be so stupid.

[JIM *turns away from* ALLAN, *who grabs* JIM *and throws him
across the room.* JIM *is stunned and disoriented*]

ALLAN Never hit me! Never hit me!

Why the hell d'you do that? I'm sorry. I'm sorry.

[ALLAN *runs over to* JIM]

Shit. You're bleeding.

JIM I musta bit my cheek. There's blood.

Get away.

ALLAN Just let me ...

JIM Get away. I'll take care of it.

327

[JIM *stumbles up, gets a cloth, and dabs at his mouth*]

ALLAN I'm sorry, man. You gonna be alright?

You shouldna hit me.

JIM You're right. That was stupid.

ALLAN Alright.

And you shouldn't be ridin' me all the time, neither. Especially about sex an' that. I mean, who the fuck do you think you are?

I mean, I know you're only doin' it 'cause you ... You're only doing it 'cause ... But I'm seventeen, for Chrissake! I'm straight.

JIM [*dabs at his lip*] Not old enough to kill yourself. Sorry.

ALLAN Come on! How many guys my age ... how many guys my age have it already?

JIM Oh, it's really catching on. You wanna be the first on your block?

ALLAN No, but ...

JIM [*very angry*] Look, I don't have time for this bullshit. When I was infected, hardly any of my friends thought they had it either, alright?

ALLAN Yeah, but ...

JIM When I was infected I figured it was just guys who fucked around a lot. Or drag queens, or leather queens, or guys who went to the baths. And you wanna know the last one? The best one? I thought it was just older guys. Like I was too young to get it.

It's always somebody else, right? Well, forget it. That is so fucking stupid.

ALLAN But still—now don't get mad or nothin'. But still— everybody who's got it, they're mostly gay, right? Or junkies or something.

JIM And what? We don't count?

ALLAN No!

JIM [*overlapping*] We deserve it?

ALLAN [*overlapping*] You know what I mean!

JIM The virus doesn't care who you fuck. Missionaries could get it.

[*Beat*]

ALLAN But me and Sherri-Lee ...

JIM What?

ALLAN We been goin' around.

JIM Right.

ALLAN We know each other.

JIM Think about it.

[*Beat*]

ALLAN I love her.

JIM I know you do. But I fell in love with the first ten guys I had
sex with. No shit. Every time, I figured that was it for life.

  I never told you what it was like, did I? When I moved down
here.

  You think Mom was fucked up when she found that slimy
little safe of yours? You should've seen her when I told her
I was gay. Next day she tried to walk in front of a bus. Really.

  She was on tranquilizers an' everything. I wanted God to kill
me. I even went for counselling at the church.

[*Beat*]

ALLAN She really tried to kill herself?

JIM Yeah. But I think she had plans for it to rebound onto me.
She'd be dead, but I'd have guilt.

ALLAN She's just so nuts, eh? Now don't get mad. I believe what
you're saying about AIDS, an' all that. It's just ... it's just like
it's the perfect excuse, eh? It's the perfect excuse for people like
Mom to tell ya not to have sex. You know what I mean?

JIM Yeah. Exactly.

Can I tell you something? I never told this to anybody else before.

[ALLAN *nods*]

Sex is slippery. [*laughs*] And I don't mean just physically. I mean, like, it's slippery about life and death.

Like, when I had sex. Like the time when I was probably infected, I already knew it could kill me.

Okay?

Like I wasn't trying to kill myself, exactly. But I didn't want to give in to all those people who were telling me it wasn't alright for me to have sex, right?

So I used condoms most of the time, but this one time ... Sorry, I never told anybody this before. This one time, I met this guy in a bar. And it was just, like—electric! So we necked a bit an' that. And by the time we went out to his truck, I already knew I didn't want to use any protection. Like, I didn't want anything to get in the way of the experience.

He looked healthy, right?

Like I was just trying to live, okay? But you know the first thing I thought when I heard about AIDS? That it'd be a really good way to commit suicide. So I was playin' the edge.

ALLAN You did it on purpose.

JIM Not exactly.

ALLAN Not exactly! What'd you just say? I always thought it was more or less an accident. I didn't know you were playing Russian roulette.

JIM I said I was riding the edge.

ALLAN Oh well, then. That makes a big difference. Why are you telling me this, anyway? I don't wanna hear it. Why don't you tell me what you did exactly? Did you fuck him or did he fuck you?

330

JIM Allan ...

ALLAN I always thought you were different. Like when guys at school'd make jokes about the West End an' that? Like they'd make jokes about faggots? I'd always tell 'em to shut up or I'd shove their fuckin' teeth down their throat. 'Cause I thought I was defending you, right? 'Cause I thought you were fuckin' different. I thought you were decent. I didn't know you were just like all the other faggots.

JIM That's enough.

ALLAN Don't tell me that's enough! I'm not finished yet! You knew it was dangerous and you still did it! How could you do that?!

JIM I didn't know what was going to happen ...

ALLAN You knew! You knew what was going to happen! You just told me. You wanted to fuck this guy and you didn't care if you killed yourself.

[*Beat.* JIM *has nothing to say*]

You killed yourself, man. You killed yourself.

[ALLAN *picks up his knapsack and starts to throw some of his junk into it*]

JIM What are you doing?

ALLAN What does it look like?

JIM Don't be stupid. Where you gonna go?
Where you gonna go?

ALLAN Fuck off.

JIM Tell me where you're going.

ALLAN Whaddyou care?

JIM Don't be stupid.

ALLAN No. I used to be stupid.
Whatever happened to, 'I'll always take care of you, Allan. I'll always be there for you, Allan'? Bullshit! [*he grabs more stuff*]

[*Beat.* JIM *tries to grab* ALLAN *by the shoulder*]

Don't …! I don't know who you are any more. I thought you were my brother.

JIM Well, fuck you too, then. Go ahead. Put your hand through another fucking window. Do it right this time.

[ALLAN *races off. He throws himself on the floor in his playing area and kicks and screams. This may be accompanied on the soundtrack by the sounds of loud music, revving engines, and squealing tires. The eruption ends when* ALLAN *is exhausted*]

Be Here Now

JIM *is in the apartment, searching for something. He finds a second sweater and puts it on. He sits and reads.* RALPH *enters, full of life. He's carrying a bag of groceries*

RALPH Hi. How ya doing?

JIM I'm freezing. I'm always bloody freezing these days. My teeth are chattering.

How's your cold?

RALPH [*shrugs*] What's the latest on Allan?

JIM Mom wants to put the cops on his tail. About the car. But I think I talked her out of it.

Sometimes I'm afraid he's going to do something really stupid. Like really stupid.

RALPH He'll come back.

[RALPH *gets a quilt and tucks it around* JIM. JIM *snuggles into it as* RALPH *sits next to him*]

JIM Your timing's really lousy, you know that? If you'd come into my life about two years earlier, I might not be in this mess.

RALPH Right. Now it's my fault.

JIM You bet.

RALPH According to all the gurus, we didn't find one another too late. We found one another just in time.

JIM Yes, Guru Ralph.

RALPH I think they've got a point. Play it as it lays, so to speak.

JIM Right.

[JIM *picks up* RALPH*'s hand and starts to suck his fingers*]

RALPH What? You're not gonna get dirty on me all of a sudden, are ya?

JIM Why not? Can you think of anything you'd rather do right now?

[JIM *kisses* RALPH]

RALPH What about my cold? I mean, in terms of opportunistic infections …

JIM Why don't you just shut up for a sec?

RALPH You really want to do this?

JIM Shut up.

[*They kiss again and start to make love*]

RALPH Oh. I've missed this.

JIM Me too.

[*More*]

Kiss-Off

SHERRI Al-Guy. I don't know where you are right now, but I want you to get this as soon as you get back. The number one thing I got to say is I don't want to see you anymore, so don't try to get in touch with me. I thought we had something—like real love—but if you loved me, then how could you just go ahead and make me feel like this? I don't get why you acted like that. And it scares me. And number two is I let you do it and that scares me worse. You know what I mean? I mean I didn't want to make love to you that night, but I let you do it. For what? Like if I give you sex, you make sure I never have to be alone. Right? Like I been so lonely. So don't try and get in touch with me anyway.

And I'm not gonna see anybody else for a while, either. So there's no other guy, alright? I don't know why guys always think that—like we can't live without it. But if I start off lonely and end up feeling like dirt ... So, it's gonna be weird not having a boyfriend for a while. Or not having sex, anyway. Some people are gonna think I'm weird.

Number three is I really do love you. But not like I wanna get back together. Just like I really hope you work it out. And me too. Wish me luck. Sherri.

Corridor

JIM enters, very sick, in hospital pyjamas and a sweater. He addresses the support group

JIM Allan came back after about two weeks on the road. We tried to talk, but it was like we'd lost the language.

Even when I got pneumonia on top of the KS, Allan didn't come to the hospital much.

Now I got something on my chest again.

I dunno. When it really, like, hits the fan, eh?—I still want Ralph to call him.

[JIM *approaches his hospital bed, attaches his IV tube, and lies down. He takes a final, bird-like look around him, then, with* RALPH*'s help, he secures his oxygen mask.* RALPH *goes into the corridor outside* JIM*'s room. He is joined by* ALLAN]

ALLAN How is he now?

RALPH They say he's right on the edge. Where've you been?

ALLAN It's hard to get in from the valley. I been busy.

[*Pause*]

RALPH He hasn't been conscious for two days. But he can still hear, I'm sure of it.

Why don't you go in?

ALLAN In a minute.

RALPH His breathing's pretty bad. They call it Cheyne-Stoking.

ALLAN Sounds like chain-smoking.

RALPH Yeah. He's been doing it for hours.

ALLAN Does it hurt?

RALPH He's on a lot of morphine.

   The doctor said he should've died a week ago.

ALLAN You're not gonna get any of his stuff, you know. I don't care what it says in his will.

   What? Aren't you gonna come back at me with some smart little fag joke?

[*Beat*]

RALPH You know what I think's really sad?

   Your brother's dying in there and you never even knew him.

[RALPH *exits*]

Hospital

JIM's room in the hospital. It's dimly lit and we can hear the sound of JIM's heart monitor. ALLAN enters

ALLAN Jim? How ya doin'? It's Al.

Ya know what Ralph just said? He said I don't even know ya. What an asshole.

Like I know, for instance, that you wouldn't want to have your hair lookin' like that. What'd they cut it with anyway, a lawnmower?

[*he checks his pockets*] No comb, so I guess I can use my hands, eh?

[*He rearranges JIM's hair, very gently*]

That's okay. Now you look a little bit more like yourself.

Ralph says you can still hear pretty good.

First thing I wanted to tell you is, I'm sorry I took off like that. But it was kind of a shock, eh? All at once. Sometimes I felt like you were with me, though. Night-times on the highway.

So your breathing's not too good, eh? That doesn't sound too comfortable.

It doesn't hurt, though, does it?

Ralph said ... Ralph said he thought you wanted to talk to me. Prob'ly wanna chew me out, right?

All that shit I said about you killin' yourself and everything. It isn't true. I guess I was just ... I dunno. Like back when

338

I was in the hospital before? It wasn't exactly like I was tryin' to kill myself either. But they were right. It woulda been a pretty good accident.

So all of a sudden, it's like you're tellin' me you're just as stupid as I am. And I just got so pissed off.

But I know you were only tellin' me 'cause ... So that's okay, eh?

So, I guess what I'm saying is, if it hurts too much to breathe an' that ...

[*Pause*]

I know I haven't been visiting much, but it's not because I don't ...

I'm just ashamed of myself, okay? You always took real good care o' me and then I turn around and treat you like shit. I guess that wasn't too mature. After what I said, callin' you a faggot an' that, I guess I figured I could never tell you how much I'm sorry. Well, I am. I'm sorry, Jimmy.

I know I'm not doin' such a great job, like o' being more responsible an' that. But I am tryin' though.

I guess what I'm trying to say is, if it hurts too much ... um ... you don't have to stick around just to take care o' me.

I know you always wanted to be, like, my dad an' that. And you been a real good dad ... You been a real good dad. But now I can take care o' myself. Okay? So don't worry. I'm gettin' a lot better at takin' care of myself.

[*Pause*]

You know what? I heard about people who said they saw lights and stuff. On the other side. And they saw people they knew there and it was like, really warm and everything? And they said that they felt, like—known, okay? Like people, or whoever was there—God or something—like he knew them and he loved them, okay?

I don't want it to hurt, okay? So if it hurts a lot, maybe you should just go wherever it is you're going. Okay? I'll hang around at this end and hold your hand until somebody grabs on on the other side. How's that?

Oh wait. Wait. I brought something.

[ALLAN *takes his Walkman from around his neck and slides the headset onto* JIM. *He puts the Walkman on* JIM*'s chest*]

Isn't that perfect? Perfect music. How many other brothers coulda taught me that?

I guess I never told you that I love you. But we knew that already, right?

Go ahead. I can take care of myself.

[*As* JIM *stops breathing and the monitor stops,* ALLAN *takes several deep breaths*]

[*End*]

Notes by the Contributors

John Alcorn

When composing the music for *Capote at Yaddo*, my first
objective was to create settings in which Sky Gilbert's lyrics
could be clearly understood. Another important consideration
was the time period. The 1940s have always signified Swing to
me. Hence the nightclub-patter style of 'Howard's Song' and
the jauntily optimistic groove of the opening and closing group
numbers, which is meant to contrast or 'set up' Sky's angry,
sardonic, and ultimately comic lyrics. (Vit Wagner of the
Toronto Star noted the 'hilariously inappropriate marriage
of style and content'—I took that as a compliment.) With
'Newton's Song' I tried to create a sort of angular elegance,
while 'Mary's Song' is a rather shameless take on Judy Garland
in the 'Born in a Trunk' era.

David Demchuk

Many gay men—myself included—have a special relationship
with pornography. It has validated our desires, deciphered our
secret code of glances and gestures, it has revealed our hidden
meeting places and intimate rituals; it has also, for various
reasons, presented us with images and texts that eroticize our
oppression, violation, compromise, and self-hatred. I wrote
Touch at a time when it was thought to be counter-productive
to be critical of our sexual materials instead of fighting to
protect them. I wrote it to ask myself why I responded with
arousal to the homophobia often present in gay porn, and if it

was possible to defy or subvert it not through censorship (which I do not support), but by re-imagining the texts, the images, by re-imagining myself, ourselves and our place in the world.

Ken Garnhum

The characters in my works have been said to be obsessive personalities; if the works themselves can be said to be obsessed with a single idea, it is the idea of 'survival.' This is particularly true of *Beuys Buoys Boys* which explores survival through the life and work of the German artist and humanist Joseph Beuys, through a childhood by the sea, and through a personal response to the AIDS epidemic. The exploration, however, does not end (nor, indeed, necessarily begin) with these titled subjects, for perhaps more than anything else, my works deny singularity and insist on the connectedness of all things. It is important to continue asking questions even after accepting the true shortage of answers. Questions, like survival, are dangerous and adventurous. Because of the abundance of questions in *Beuys Buoys Boys* the reader/viewer may find themselves at the occasional crossroads, wondering which path to follow. Cervantes, in *Don Quixote*, said, 'There are two roads; both of them lead nowhere; but one of them has a heart.' My advice—as always—is keep moving and, wherever possible, keep heart.

Sky Gilbert

Capote at Yaddo is an odd little beast. I've written many stage biographies of gay artists (Constantine Cavafy, Pier Paolo Pasolini and others); they were not musicals. I've written many musicals, but they have usually involved drag (*Suzi Goo: Private Secretary, Lola Starr Builds Her Dream Home*). Maybe this is what makes the piece so special for me; I've written nothing like it before. It's supposed to be about love and illusion, which is why Arvin gets the last word instead of our 'little vain genius.' Since there is no dedication I will say (mysteriously) that the young Capote and the older Arvin are very much based on a boy and a man of my acquaintance. A note to the players: don't try to imitate Capote's irritating voice all through the play—an imitation of Capote is only required, as indicated, in his second monologue.

And then there's the issue of whether my piece is historically accurate. Well it isn't (it's always been my goal in these biographies to search for the essence of celebrated people, not the details)! It is true that Capote was at Yaddo in 1946 and that he had a long affair that lasted several years with Newton Arvin. However, at this time Mary Arvin had divorced her husband long ago. Putting Mary at Yaddo gave my play added conflict. My source and the inspiration for the play is Gerald Clarke's excellent biography *Capote*. It should be noted that Newton Arvin died in a small New England town soon after a scandal erupted over the discovery of his pornography collection. At age sixty he was forced out of the closet and seemed at the time to be a happier man for it. But I think that's another play ...

Daniel MacIvor

In 1989 at Le Festival de Théâtre des Amériques in Montreal, I was a performer in DNA Theatre's *Hamlet*, a nine-hour performance epic. On one of our very few nights off Ken McDougall and I saw a production of *Merz Opera* by Montreal's Théâtre Ubu. It was the kind of work I had been experimenting with for some time but was reticent to produce because I was not sure if it had any reality outside my own imagination. But here it was on-stage before me: a perfect synthesis of performance and text; no sense of separation

343

between what the actor was saying, how he appeared to feel about what he was saying, how he said it, and how he moved. I went away and finished work on *2-2-Tango* (which began as a nearly impenetrable performance-poem). *2-2-Tango* comes from an obsession with the beauty and banality of language and a belief that Theatre is about Performance. (Of course, 'Performance' has nothing to do with what we have come to understand as 'acting' ... but that is another rant entirely.) *2-2-Tango* is a product and part of a New Theatre, a Theatre of the present moment which happens *now* and acknowledges the space between the stage and the seats. It is essential that this be part of any production of this piece.

Harry Rintoul

I get asked a lot, 'What is it about?'

My stock answer is, 'It's about love.' Which is always part of it and is, at the very least, an answer. But a stock answer just the same. Is there any way I can avoid answering this question?

In the plays I have written I have set out to tackle the problems people have in communicating. Communication is a gift, and the fact that we constantly abuse that gift amazes and fascinates me. What we require and what we want are often most easily obtained by asking. But so often we do not ask; we avoid. The problem is clearly defined for those who know what they want, have the ability to ask directly, and choose not to. But how do you tell someone what you want or need when you don't know how? When what you're used to is not asking, making do, getting by? The reasons for this behaviour and its acceptance are learned. Don't ask because you won't get it. Don't ask because you'll be shot down in flames. Don't ask because you're not worth it, and why would anyone fall in love with someone like you? So instead of asking you lash out, strike out, hit and destroy, or fall silent and keep it all inside because there are no rules to the game. This has more to do with self-esteem and confidence than it has to do with love.

Brave Hearts is about wanting to not be alone. It is about loneliness. It is about self-esteem and self-confidence. It is about having a future and no control, and control over no future. It is about positive role models. Truth. It is about being honest. To yourself. To others. It is about chance and memory. It is about circumstance. And circumstances. It is about the nightly parade played out in bars and dark city streets, the lonely and the pained looking for the free and unrestrained, the dark seeking the light. It is about not living in the city. About not having a community or a ghetto.

It is about forgetting the past and living in the future.

It is about, 'Ya wanna know why I came here tonight? I'll tell you if you're still interested …'

And that has more to do with love.

Colin Thomas

In the original commission for *Flesh and Blood*, I was asked to write a show about AIDS that could tour to both high-school students and the general community. I immediately (and unconsciously) interpreted 'the general community' to mean gay men. I wanted to address the gay male community specifically, because my own relationship to AIDS is so bound up in my gay sexuality. To address the needs of both groups I chose two themes: consistent condom use and homophobia.

Teenagers especially use condoms inconsistently, so that theme is urgent. The theme of homophobia is obviously more complex. Teenagers use homophobia as a way of denying their vulnerability to the disease. ('If it only happens to subhumans it can't happen to me.') For gay men, internalized homophobia teaches us that our essential, sexual natures are so hateful that

345

ostracism, even to the point of abandonment and death, is just punishment.

I am personally terrified of being left alone to die. In approaching my specific fears in this play, I hope that my themes begin to become universal. When the characters in *Flesh and Blood* face the horror of their own aloneness they start to release themselves from guilt and addictive behaviours; they begin to sense their inherent, independent worthiness, and feel the freedom to love one another. For gay men, for teenagers, for everybody who is exposed to this play, that is my hope: that they will be free to know themselves, and that their love will be taken to its fullest expression.

Notes on the Contributors

John Alcorn
Toronto-born John Alcorn is a singer-songwriter whose
performing style has been described as combining a 'Cole Porter
finesse with a hurtin' yowl' (*Rites*). At the tender age of fifteen
he began his involvement with the theatre world and has, in
the ensuing years, worked as an actor, director, musical director
and arranger. The score for *Capote at Yaddo: A Very Gay Little
Musical* is his first attempt at composing for the theatre.

David Demchuk
David Demchuk's other plays include *If Betty Should Rise*,
published in Coach House Press's anthology *Canadian Brash;
Stay*, produced by New York's Mass Transit Theatre Company;
Alaska, a CBC Radio Morningside Drama; and *Mattachine*,
produced by Proving Ground Theatre at the 1991 Fringe of
Toronto festival. *Touch* shared the 1986 Dora Mavor Moore
Award for Innovation and Artistic Excellence. Demchuk's
prose sequence *Seven Dreams* is published in chapbook form
by the Pink Dog Press. He lives in Toronto.

Ken Garnhum
Ken Garnhum has written nine theatre works since 1986,
including three full-length one-person pieces: *Surrounded By
Water* (1991), *Beuys Buoys Boys* (1989) and *How Many Saints
Can Sit Around* (1987). Other works include: *Building a
Postmodern Birdhouse* (1986) and *The Bicycle Was Red* (1991).

He has designed sets and costumes for most of his own works and for other small theatre companies, as well as having worked as an associate with many of Canada's top designers. From 1989-1991 he was Playwright-in-Residence at Toronto's Tarragon Theatre where, during the writing of *Beuys Buoys Boys*, he was also an associate artist of the Tarragon-Chalmers playwrights' unit. *Beuys Buoys Boys* was nominated for two Dora Mavor Moore Awards in 1989: Best New Play and Best Set Design. Garnhum studied graphic design and visual art and continues to produce drawings and objects mainly, but not exclusively, for his performance works. Born on Prince Edward Island, he divides his time between Earnescliffe, P.E.I, Toronto, and Stratford.

Sky Gilbert

Playwright, poet, actor, or drag queen extraordinaire ... Sky Gilbert is one of Canada's most controversial artistic forces. As the co-founder and artistic director of Buddies In Bad Times Theatre, Gilbert has written and directed his own hit plays: *Pasolini/Pelosi, The Dressing Gown* (published by the Playwrights Union of Canada in August 1989), *Drag Queens on Trial, Ban This Show, The Post Man Rings Once,* and *Capote at Yaddo.* In keeping with the nature of his work Gilbert has been outspoken on issues affecting lesbian and gay communities. By nurturing and inspiring other young artists, Gilbert helps to ensure a strong and alternative cultural voice in Canada through Buddies' *Rhubarb!* and QueerCulture festivals. For the Shaw Festival Gilbert directed *Anything Goes,* and *Salome,* and was the assistant director for the original Shaw Festival production of *Cyrano de Bergerac.* Other critically-acclaimed productions directed by Gilbert include: *Treatment* for Another Stage, and *How I Wonder What You Are* for Theatre Direct. Gilbert received the Pauline McGibbon Award for Directing in 1985, and a Dora Mavor Moore Award for Best New Play, Small Theatre Division for *The Whore's Revenge* in 1989.

Daniel MacIvor

Daniel MacIvor was born in Cape Breton, Nova Scotia in 1962. He studied Theatre at Dalhousie University in Halifax and George Brown College in Toronto. He is an actor, director, producer, writer and artistic director of Da Da Kamera. His plays include *See Bob Run, Wild Abandon, House, Never Swim Alone* and *Jump*. He has been nominated five times for the Chalmers New Canadian Play Award: in 1988 for *See Bob Run*, in 1990 for the collective creation *White Trash Blue Eyes*, and in 1991 for *Never Swim Alone, 2-2-Tango*, and *House*, which won.

Harry Rintoul

Harry Rintoul was born in 1956 in Canmore, Alberta and was moved to Winnipeg a couple of months later because, as he was told, there was work in Winnipeg. He began his writing career in 1983. His plays include *refugees*, produced by Kam Theatre in Thunder Bay in 1987 and published by Blizzard Publishing in 1988; *Montana; 1919; Together, Forever, Between Then and Now* and *life & times*. *Brave Hearts* was a 1991 Dora Mavor Moore Award Nominee for Outstanding New Play, Small Theatre Division. Rintoul has written for CBC Radio and currently divides his time between writing and performing the duties of artistic director/producer for Theatre Projects Manitoba Inc. As much as he likes living in the city he'd much rather be living on a ranch or farm somewhere taking care of animals and watching things grow.

Colin Thomas

Trained as an actor at the Bristol Old Vic Theatre School and the University of British Columbia, Colin Thomas turned to playwriting when he got sick of merely interpreting other people's ideas. As an actor he often worked with political and experimental companies such as Touchstone Theatre, Headlines Theatre, and Green Thumb Theatre for Young People. When he began playwriting he felt that he found his true voice in speaking to the issues of abandoned and ignored youth. Although he continues to write for young people and their families his audiences are getting older. Maintaining a twenty-year age gap with his market, he may soon be writing solely for adults. Thomas is also Theatre Critic for the *Georgia Straight*, contributes theatre criticism to CBC Radio, and writes poems for *Sesame Street*.

Robert Wallace
Robert Wallace has been writing for and about the theatre for over twenty years. Of the five stage plays he wrote during the 1970s, *No Deposit No Return* premiered in New York and *'67* was published by the Playwrights Union of Canada. During the 1980s, besides regularly speaking about theatre on CBC Radio, he wrote and produced ten feature documentaries on the arts for CBC *Ideas*. Editor of *Canadian Theatre Review* from 1982-1988, he has written widely for newspapers, magazines and scholarly journals. As drama editor for Coach House Press, his numerous editions of Canadian plays have won five Governor General's Awards for drama. His own books include *The Work: Conversations with Canadian Playwrights* (with Cynthia Zimmerman), and *Producing Marginality: Theatre and Criticism in Canada*. Wallace lives in Toronto where he is a Professor of English at Glendon College, York University.

Editor for the Press: Robert Wallace
Cover Design: Clare McGoldrick / Reactor
Cover Photo: Dina Almeida
Printed in Canada

Coach House Press
401 (rear) Huron Street
Toronto, Canada
M5S 2G5